You've Got to be Kidding!

A Moore Family Odyssey, Book Two

Connie Moore

Belleville, Ontario, Canada

Me? An Australian Farmer? You've Got to be Kidding!
Copyright © 2003, Connie Moore

All Rights Reserved. No part of this publication may be reproduced, stored in a retrieval system or transmitted in any form or by any means—electronic, mechanical, photocopy, recording or any other—except for brief quotations in printed reviews, without the prior permission of the author.

National Library of Canada Cataloguing in Publication

Moore, Connie, 1930-
    Me? An Australian farmer? You've got to be kidding! / Connie Moore.

(A Moore family odyssey ; Bk. 2)
ISBN 1-55306-637-5

    1. Moore, Connie, 1930- 2. Farmers' spouses--Australia--Biography. 3. Farm life--Australia. I. Title. II. Series: Moore family odyssey Bk. 2.

DU117.2.M66A3 2003   630'.92   C2003-905852-2

For more information or
to order additional copies, please contact:

Connie Moore
9701 East Hwy. 25, #176
Belleview FL 34420
Phone or Fax: (352) 347-5492

Epic Press is an imprint of *Essence Publishing,* a Christian Book Publisher dedicated to furthering the work of Christ through the written word. For more information, contact: 20 Hanna Court, Belleville, Ontario, Canada K8P 5J2. Phone: 1-800-238-6376   Fax: (613) 962-3055.   E-mail: publishing@essencegroup.com Internet: www.essencegroup.com

Table of Contents

Acknowledgements 5
Meet the Family 7
Preface 9
Prologue 11

1. A Farmer's Life 13
2. Getting Acquainted 23
3. Special Events 29
4. It's a Different World 35
5. Broken-Downsville 45
6. An Australian Baby 53
7. Unforgettable Events 59
8. The Shipment Arrives 65
9. The Saga of Smokey and Big Red 71
10. Thoughts from the Farmer's Wife 81
11. Changing Crops 89
12. Christmas Down Under 99
13. Stradbroke Adventures 107
14. Smelling the Roses 115
15. The Way Things Are 123

16. Unsung Heroes 129
17. Going Places and Doing Things . 135
18. Stepping Out at Easter Time . . . 141
19. The Winds of Change 149
20. The Birthdays 157

Acknowledgements

Special thanks to my seven children who were always ready to fill in the blanks.

To Tim Rankin of the Macintosh Users Group for keeping my computer system happy.

To John Massey, graphic designer, for his sketch of the book cover.

To my husband, Bill, a valuable resource of facts and figures. My on-site critic and greatest supporter. He has donned his new "hat" as Public Relations Manager with confidence and charm.

Meet the family

Meet the Family

RUSTY—Fourteen years old with red hair, freckles and broad shoulders. Sets a good example as the family leader. Loves hunting and fishing.

MICKEY—Twelve-year-old blonde organizer. Has a flair for interior design and building. Enjoys taking care of the younger ones.

SKIPPY—Ten-year-old brunette. Much harder to understand. He's at the top of his class in school. Excels at sports, like his dad.

TIA—Seven-year-old dainty blonde. Good at studies, determined and independent. Loves to sew. Takes good care of the younger girls.

PAM—Four-year-old blonde. Tiny in build, the most curious of all the children. Pam's the older half of a dynamic duo.

Jackie—Two and a half years old. With her strawberry blond hair and a smattering of freckles, is hard to resist. She's the other half of the dynamic duo.

Topper—makes his debut in this book. You will love him, as we all do.

Preface

IN THIS BOOK I HAVE ENDEAVORED TO render the truth as accurately as possible. Even though this is my story, it includes many other people who played major or minor roles. In some cases my interpretation of events will perhaps differ from another's perspective. A few names have been changed because of circumstances.

Dialogue and incidents are reported to the best of my recollection. Although I cannot be certain every quote is entirely accurate word for word, the thoughts, ideas and circumstances of the story have been preserved.

—*Connie Moore*

Russell Island

The largest of the R.K.L.M. group, Russell Island is a subtropical haven in Tranquil Moreton Bay
* Fiddler's Green

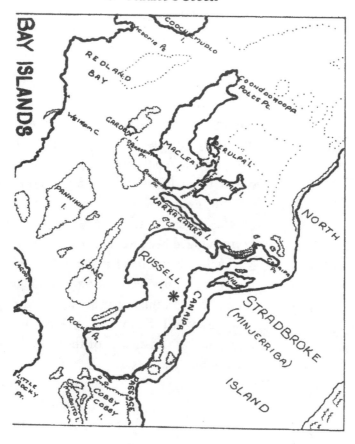

Prologue

ONCE UPON A TIME... NO, THIS ISN'T A fairy tale, although it may sound like one. Since childhood, Connie Moore had dreamed of visiting far away places. In a dream come true, she was living in Japan in the early 1960s. In three years, at the age of thirty-seven, Bill, her Navy career husband, would retire. Serving with the Office of Naval Intelligence, he made friends at the Australian Embassy. "Australia is a great place to live," they told him.

One day, when he and Connie were discussing where they would retire, Bill suggested, "We could move to Australia."

"You've got to be kidding!" Connie responded with raised eyebrows. "I've always wanted to see the world—but Australia! That's a long way from home."

Transferred back to the States, they noticed a difference in America. Children had rooms full of toys but lacked a sense of responsibility. Captivated by television, they were missing the challenge of outside play. Connie and Bill wanted more traditional values for their family.

After months of studying about the country, the decision was made. To Australia they would go. Friends and relatives were stunned at the idea of taking six children so far away, but slowly became resigned.

On May 24th, 1963, the Moore family sailed into Sydney Harbor. They were greeted by a TV cameraman and reporter who wanted to interview them. Much to their surprise, they were a "news item."

After an adventurous trek across Australia and back, they settled in Queensland. Searching for a family farm, Bill discovered the Moreton Bay Islands. Eleven months later, they were on the ferry to Russell Island... followed by a barge carrying their furniture.

Chapter One

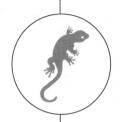

A Farmer's Life

They say a farmer's life is a lot of hard work with little pay and perhaps they're right. We have close to twenty acres, most of it cleared. There are two acres of banana trees and some small crops—marrows, pumpkin and cucumbers. The rest is just waiting for us to do something with it. At the top of a small hill are two acres of woods, mostly gums and cypress trees. An ideal place for active young boys to work off surplus energy.

Our irrigation well is just on the other side of the hill. From there you can peek through the trees to see the bay down below. The well is sixty-feet deep and has a huge pump—the type you see scattered in the Texas oil fields. The pump sends water through aluminum pipes to the crops. During planting season it's a constant chore moving the twenty foot long pipes from field to field.

When the pump motor is running, it is so loud we can hear it down at the house. That's fine. It's only when the noise stops that we get nervous. Silence means the pump is either broken down, or the engine has run out of petrol. These big machines and numerous details of farm life overwhelm me. There is so much to cope with!

Imagine not having an electric company! We generate our own power with a small diesel generator. It's not practical to run it all the time, so we work with what we have.

I'm gradually getting accustomed to the wood stove and we're eating a little bit earlier. When the children come home from school, their first chore is to find enough dry wood to fill the old green wood box. A full wood box means we can cook dinner and have enough hot water for baths. Our slow combustion stove has a built in water tank connected to our main water supply. Not necessarily a modern convenience, but it sure beats heating buckets of water over a fire in the back yard!

I caution the boys, "If you want an early dinner, don't bring me any wet wood, or green wood."

"Why not?" Skippy asks.

"Because," I answer, tapping him on the end of his nose., "wet wood is so full of moisture, it requires lots of kindling, and lots of time for it to get hot enough to cook food. Green wood doesn't want to burn at all!" It had taken many evenings of late late dinners to teach me that bit of information. I was delighted to pass it on to the next generation.

"Okay," Skippy grins, promising to look for dry wood.

Using American recipes in Australia is another hurdle I had not anticipated. Basics like flour, sugar and syrup are processed differently than in the States. It requires a lot of substituting. But I'm learning to adapt my recipes to Australian ingredients. Mother's Day was my biggest triumphant so far. I served Bill's favorite dessert, an "American" pumpkin pie that tasted like American pumpkin pie!

Rearranging the kitchen pantry one day, I came across a strange looking piece of equipment. About twelve inches high, it had long skinny legs and a fat middle. "What's this for?" I asked Bill.

"I don't know," he said with a puzzled look.

"Well, I'll just put it back for now. It might come in handy one day."

A few weeks later, after the children had left for school, there was a knock on the door. I opened it to a stranger. He was too nicely dressed to be an islander. Besides—he had shoes on. Seeing my confusion, he explained that he was a Methodist minister from the mainland. "I've come over to visit the island folk," he said.

Relieved, I invited him in. "We don't see many strangers on the island this time of day," I told him. I apologized for not being able to offer him a cup of tea. "The fire is out in the wood stove and I don't know how to start it."

"Don't you have a primus?" he asked, in a tone of voice that conveyed, "everyone" has a primus.

"What's that?" I asked.

"It has a round tank like this," he made a circle with his hands, "and it has legs about this high."

I reached into the pantry and lifted out our mystery gadget. "Is this it?"

His face brightened. Right then and there, I got a lesson on how to start a primus. "Do you have kerosene and metho?"

"What's metho?" I asked.

He looked at me with a grin, "Metho is like alcohol. Australians use a lot of it."

I ran downstairs to fetch the kerosene and found a bottle of metho. Well supplied, he began to teach. "You fill the tank with kerosene and put some metho in the little cup at the top. Light the metho with a match and just before it burns out, pump this knob. Then you flick the starter switch and presto! you have a one burner gas stove."

He looked up, beaming at me as the flames came to life. That little primus revolutionized our way of living! The water boiled quickly and we enjoyed a visit over a hot cup of tea. I listened to his news of the island group and the outside world.

World news was something Bill and I knew little about. The radio only gave us brief sketches every two hours. As a rule, we read the comics before we checked the front page of the newspaper. It always surprised me to find, that the world was able to rotate—in space—without our constant attention.

I had discovered that learning to cope with a kerosene refrigerator was more important than keeping the world on course. If the flame was too low it dripped. If the flame burned too high, it smoked. I could smell it all over the house. Bill had tried everything he knew to do.

"Perhaps Ian will be able to help," I suggested. "Hypatia called to let us know they would be coming over to Russell on Sunday."

"I hope so," Bill sighed as he wiped his hands and slid the fuel tank back into place. "It will be nice to see them. We had a lot of fun when we visited them on Macleay."

We had met the Robinsons on one of our early ferry crossings. "Do come over to Macleay to see us," Hypatia had invited, in her delightful French accent. She was a beautiful woman from Jersey, an island in the English Channel. "We live in a little doll house," she explained, "you must come see it." We did, and had a lovely visit in the house they had designed and built themselves. It was small but adequate and beautifully decorated. When we left, they had promised to visit us on Russell.

When Sunday arrived, Bill brought them up from the jetty. We settled in the living room to chat over a cup of tea. I apologized for not being able to offer them a cold drink, "The kerosene refrigerator just won't cooperate," I sighed.

Ian unfolded his six foot frame, stood up, nodded to Bill and said, "Let's go have a look." They disappeared into the kitchen.

Sensing my concern, Hypatia assured me, "Ian has spent a lot of time dealing with that kind of refrigerator." I could hear the scrape of the kerosene tank being removed and their steps going down stairs. I hoped they were taking it to the shed to fix it.

"Probably to clean it." Hypatia offered. Since these things are new to him, Bill might not know that the wick has to be cleaned regularly."

In a short time they were back in the kitchen. I could hear the tank being replaced and the men making satisfying noises. After a few tense minutes I heard the refrigerator door being opened. "It's working!" Bill exclaimed, "the freezer is getting cold." I breathed a sigh of relief.

"It's wonderful to have friends who brighten the lives of the ignorant," I smiled. "Especially friends with experience in reviving ancient objects."

Hypatia laughed, "We, too, had to learn."

The refrigerator freezing compartment, just big enough to hold two ice cube trays, was put to good use. The next morning I mixed full-cream powdered milk, sugar, gelatin and fresh bananas to freeze as ice cubes. Just before dinner I put the frozen cubes in my mixer bowl to thaw slightly. After we ate Bill slipped out to start the generator.

"Guess what we're having for dessert," I teased the kids.

Rusty was the first to guess, "Just fruit as usual."

"Did you learn to bake a cake in that stove?" Mickey asked hopefully.

"Ice cream," Pam shouted.

"You're crazy," Tia scorned.

Bill came back and kept them guessing while I whipped the ice cubes into a smooth delicious ice cream.

"Hey, Pam was right," Skippy said, "how did she know?"

"Pam always does," Rusty observed, licking his spoon.

Over a period of time we created enough flavors to compete with Baskin Robbins. We served the ice cream after dinner in the children's milk glasses—for two good reasons. It encouraged them to finish their milk and they had less dishes to wash. In a family of eight that's an important point.

We couldn't have created a better dessert. The extra calcium contributed to their strong bones and teeth, and also, to a good night's sleep. It was probably the reason, they never went back into the kitchen during the evening hours looking for a snack.

Keeping them in clean clothes became ludicrous. Most islanders had washers with kerosene motors. We had an old electric wringer-type model with two speeds. "The best thing about our washer is the lever to drain it," Mickey boasted. "Some people have to empty theirs with a bucket."

Unfortunately, the spring that held the rollers in place was missing. Instead of rolling through, the clothes wrapped themselves tightly around the wringer. I needed one hand to feed the clothes, another to pull them through on the other side, and a third to hold the wringer clamp. Doesn't add up, does it? I've never yet met anyone with three hands.

"I'm just not suited for this kind of work!" I protested during a morning laundry session. I yelled for Bill, "Come help me untangle these things!" Besides the problem with the wringer, the machine sometimes just quit. Like Bill when his tractor stops, I was ready to give up and go home to the States.

For two weeks we did the laundry by hand with a scrub board we had bought in Japan. "It's great to be so well equipped for emergencies," I said trying to look at the brighter side. "We even have two antique, seven-pound flat irons that I hope *never* have to use," I muttered, with my fingers crossed.

"They've been bookends for years," Bill grinned. "But around here you never know. It always pays to be prepared."

Luckily, we have neighbors blessed with a talent for fixing things. If anything breaks down—and on our farm that's everything—there is usually someone around who knows how to repair it. Tom Hamlin, who is sixty-five and has a bad heart, is one of those clever fellows. "I raised four boys by myself," he told me the first time we met. "The youngest, Jerry, is the same age as your Rusty. He's the only one at home now, the others have grown and gone." Tom is handy with machines and always has an interesting tale to tell.

The day he came by to visit, I poured out my sad story. "The washing machine is broken down and everything is dirty, dirty, dirty."

"Righto!" he grinned, "I'll have a go at it." That's Australian for, "I'll try to fix it for you." He tinkered a while, discovered the problem and had it running before the afternoon was up. I was thrilled!

"What do I owe you?" I asked, willing to pay whatever.

He nodded at a pile of fresh carrots Bill had just brought in from the field, "A bunch of those would take care of it," he said. "And the next time I go to town I'll get a replacement spring for your wringer."

"Please do," I said, jumping up and down inside. God was smiling down on us.

Not long after that crisis, it became evident that something was wrong with the hot water system. The water had slowed to a trickle. It took ages to do dishes or run water for baths.

Bill came into the kitchen shaking his head, "I don't know what the problem is," he said. "Something is plugged up somewhere. I've dismantled the pipes several times and I can't find anything wrong."

"How about the tanks?" I asked.

"They're okay, I checked them for leaks."

"Did you look inside to see if there is enough water?"

"Gosh," he looked surprised. "I'm so used to city water I didn't think of that. I'm sure we have plenty of water, but I'll look, since it hasn't rained for a while." The tanks were on a high platform on the kitchen side of the house to catch rain water from the roof. Bill jumped from the railing over to the tank stand. He quickly discovered, that three one-thousand gallon tanks of water were a drop in the bucket as far as the Moore family was concerned. The tanks were almost empty!

"What can we do?" I moaned, trying not panic. "We have to have water."

"I'll try get the irrigation pump going," he said heading for the door. "If I start it, I'll run a pipeline down to the house to fill the tanks. See if you can find the boys. I'll need them to help me carry the pipe sections." Grabbing his tool box, he ran up to the well and puttered with the irrigation motor until the pump started.

When I heard the noise, I sent the boys up to move the pipes for their dad. They were thrilled with such an important job to do. One more crisis had been met and averted! "If it's worry that turns hair gray, this island living will do it for me," I announced to the empty kitchen.

To conserve water, baths were only four inches deep. The girls shared the first tub starting with the cleanest and ending with the dirtiest. Bill and I took turns in the second tubful. (Happily, since I was the cleanest, I was always first.) As long as the weather was good, the boys showered downstairs in an enclosed space under the tank stand.

Just a few days after Bill filled the tanks it rained. We were overwhelmed with water. The tanks were full and excess water was running down into the back yard. *That's the way with water,* I thought, *too little or too much. What a shame to waste it.*

Suddenly, I had a brilliant idea! I stoked up the stove, heated the holding tank and poured myself a **full** bath. Laying back in the tub I savored the luxury. What a wonderful feeling, to know that the tanks were full to overflowing. And, if necessary, we could always fill them up from the well. How utterly relaxing. I lifted handfuls of suds and let them drip slowly through my fingers. I felt more secure than I had since we left the States.

Good feelings never seem to last long around this place though. The next time the tanks were low the pump motor wouldn't start. It had to be dismantled and sent across the water to Brisbane for repairs. All I needed was something else to worry about. Will the baby have clean laundry when it arrives? How will we cook without water, or take baths? Or wash dishes, or cook meals?

Fortunately, we still had water left in one tank when the pump came back a few days later. "I'll get the pump going right away and fill up the tanks," Bill said. By early afternoon he came in with a good report, "the tanks are full."

Relieved, but exhausted, I laid down for an afternoon nap. Suddenly a great crash startled me awake. "What happened?" I yelled, rushing out to the landing.

Bill shouted back over the roar of a thousand gallons of water cascading down into the back yard, "One of the tanks burst!"

I sank down on the top step. "Now, we only have two tanks. What's next," I cried.

Chapter Two

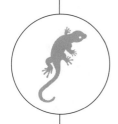

Getting Acquainted

Russell Island provided a haven for all sorts of people. It boasted twenty-five families plus weekenders. Rural life at its best. Half the school children, indeed—half the population—went barefoot most of the time. We had always been taught to wear shoes because of parasites in the soil. Apparently this did not apply in the islands. The children loved leaving their shoes behind. Eventually, the bottoms of their feet became as tough as leather.

Many of the houses, ours was one of them, were built up on stilts. "They build them high to keep the termites from eating the foundations," Mr. Wilson, the shopkeeper, explained. "Besides, the shade underneath keeps the whole house cooler in the summer."

"Then, I guess I shouldn't complain about going up and down stairs all the time," I laughed.

He grinned. "It's said that you live in the best house on the island. It's a typical Australian house, with wide verandas around three sides for shade and coolness. As families grow, parts of the veranda get converted into rooms, like your house."

We had two large bedrooms with three small bedrooms along the veranda. The living room and dining room were large. The kitchen was smaller with few cupboards balanced by a walk-in pantry. We had a bathroom with only the sink and tub. The rest of the bathroom (the WC, or privy) was down in the back yard. The laundry area was on a cement slab under the house where the mosquitoes and spiders lived.

Another challenge was learning the language. In the States, English is spoken in a northern twang or a southern drawl. The Australian lingo added a whole new dimension. "Owyergoin mate, orright?" was a simple "Hello, how are you?" A "bloke" translated to "a guy." "My mate" was not necessarily the person you were married to, it described a good friend. "Righto" meant "okay." "Littlies" were children under four-years-old. "Fair dinkum" meant "really?"

On the ferry one day, I overheard a discussion of the weather. "We crop a fair bit of it," one fellow said. I understood he was telling his friend, "We get quite a lot of bad weather." Another "bloke" on the ferry rationalize that if the mangrove trees were removed from the water's edge, all the mud would wash away and white sand would rise to the top. I didn't see how that could happen, but I liked the idea.

My favorite one was hearing them explain that if the boat sank, the water was shallow enough to walk ashore. "That may be true," I chuckled to myself. "But you had better stick to the mud banks. Even then, you might sink out of sight in the gooshy black mud."

Gradually we put names and faces together. Most people were addressed with the formal "Mr." or "Mrs." One of the few people with a nickname was seventy-year-old Butch. A white-haired bachelor and the island alcoholic. He lived a short way down the road from us, and occasionally dropped in for a visit. Sometimes drunk, sometimes sober—it was often hard to tell which. One morning he came by with a huge bouquet of flowers and a big bag of green beans from his garden. Handing me the flowers, he said with a courtly bow, "These are for a lovely lady." I received them with a courtesy and a "Thank you, sir." Butch was intelligent and full of information. I never knew him to be unkind. We shared many lively discussions about human nature and world events.

Mr. Milband, about the same age as Butch, was a slender fellow with a quick gait. He lived down the hill from us and walked past several times a day. Known as the "island newspaper," he made it a practice to meet every boat to garner news. As he made his rounds he kept everyone informed. Mr. Milband loved children and usually had several tagging along behind him.

Miss Watts, a tiny lady with skin browned and weathered by the sun, was over seventy years old. She was well versed on any subject and a walking encyclopedia on the flora and fauna of Australia. She lived alone in a little house at the bottom of the hill, sharing it with her pets—who happened to be a flock of chickens.

One day, Tia came home from Miss Watts' house gingerly carrying an egg. "See what Miss Watts gave me," she grinned.

"What's this," I asked pointing to a little piece of paper stuck on the shell.

"That's a patch," Tia explained. "It had a hole in it. Maybe the chicken pecked it, I don't know. But Miss Watts fixed it." Never, ever, in my life, have I seen a patched egg. Where on earth but Russell Island!

Mrs. Edwards, who lived just beyond Miss Watts, drove back and forth in an open-topped, vintage touring-car. The distinctive chug chug of its motor announced her coming and going. "My husband is too ill to work," she told me. "My granddaughter and I take care of the farm." Mrs. Edwards, a great organizer and hard worker, was brisk and to the point.

The Routledges, Curtis and Daphne, owned a farm on the opposite side of the road going towards the jetty. They were among the few people we called by first names. Their daughter was Rusty's age. Two younger boys were Mickey and Skippy's ages. Curtis was an excellent farmer, and became our number one reference person when we ran into problems. He was also a whiz at mechanics and loved to tinker with motors. Fortunately for us, he was always willing to help in repairing our break-downs. "Can I pay you something?" Bill offered many times.

"No, no," Curtis insisted, "I just like to help out." Finally, Bill settled the issue, by volunteering a day's work for Curtis when he needed it.

Mr. and Mrs. Graham lived beyond the Routledges, opposite the two-room school house. Jim was the head teacher, while Connie taught primary grades and music classes. They had two boys, Jimmy, who was in Mickey's grade and Michael, who was in first grade. The Grahams set the tone of the island. They kept people focused on the good things.

In early spring I noticed that their lawn looked shaggy and unkempt. "That's strange," I thought. "They're always such tidy people. I wonder if their mower is broken down like ours." When I passed their house about a week later the lawn was a sea of blue lupines. I complimented Mrs. Graham on the flowers. "Oh," she said, "they grow wild. In a few weeks the blossoms will be finished and we'll go back to cutting the grass."

Later she invited us to her house for a "Sing." She explained that every once in a while a group of islanders got together around the piano, for an evening of singing old favorite songs. "Bill and I would love to come," I said without hesitation, "singing and dancing are my favorite things to do."

The night of the Sing we arrived a little early. Before going into the living room, Bill and I stopped to have a chat with the men, who were gathered in the kitchen. Since I had studied so much about farming, I welcomed an opportunity to discuss farm practices. Actually, I'd much rather talk farming with men than recipes with women.

Later, everyone gathered around the piano to sing old songs. "Oh Susanna," "Don't Sit Under the Apple Tree," "The White Cliffs of Dover" and "This is the Army Mister Jones" were a familiar part of our growing up years. We knew them well. The evening awakened fond memories of the way America used to be.

After a few more visits with the islanders, I realized that women socialize with women in one room, and men "yabber" with men in another room. "Oh oh," I told Bill,

"No more farm talk with the men for me. We've found a common music bond with Australians, and an uncommon difference between men and women."

"Fair dinkum," Bill said practicing his Aussie drawl. "I reckon things are bit different down-under."

Chapter Three

Special Events

THE NEXT MORNING PAM AND JACKIE came running into the kitchen. "Mommy, Mommy, we're going with Daddy to get the mail."

"That's good," I said watching Bill roll up a burlap bag and tuck it under his arm. "What's that for?" I asked, pointing to the sack.

"That's my tucker bag," he grinned. "I read a lot about Australians and tucker bags but I didn't know what they were until now. 'Tucker' means food and a burlap sack is what they use to carry it home in."

"You are a fund of information," I said waving goodbye.

It wasn't long before I heard the clatter of feet coming up the stairs. "What's new?" I asked, as he handed me the mail and began to unload the food from his tucker bag.

"Something special," he announced. "Sunday, there is going to be a picnic for everyone. It's over at Macleay Island and we've been invited."

"Do we need to fix a picnic lunch?" I asked, thinking ahead.

"They said not to bring anything."

I didn't know what to expect but it sounded like fun. The children were thrilled at the prospect of an outing.

Early Sunday morning, we walked down to the jetty to join the crowd waiting for the boat. Jack Noyes, the skipper, was making a special free run to take people from the other islands to the event. "Every year," Jack explained, as he steered the boat into the channel, "we have our annual picnic over on Macleay Island. We chose Macleay because it has the largest sandy beach. There'll be lots for the tykes to do there."

The trip was short. Everyone was in a festive mood as they left the ferry and climbed into cars and trucks. The beach was two miles away over bumpy roads. I was politely offered the most comfortable seat in one of the cars, because of my "condition." With the new baby only a few weeks away, I accepted gladly.

When we arrived, a Sand-Garden Competition was already in progress. We walked along a stretch of white sand beach dotted with shells. Contestants were being creative with rocks, shells and flowers. There were separate categories for children and adults.

The children's gardens were supposed to represent a poem or nursery rhyme. "I'm going to make a Tom Thumb village for little people," Mickey said, smoothing a good sized area. "The poem will be *Little Tommy Tittlemouse*."

Rusty unpacked his fishing gear and rigged his line. "I'm ready," he said, wading out to join the fishing contest.

Tia met a friend from school and they went off to play in the water with Skippy. A couple of teenagers appeared out of nowhere and asked permission to take care of Pam and Jackie. We couldn't believe our ears. Teenagers taking care of little ones—voluntarily? I liked that idea. Jackie and Pam thought it was great, too. Off they went chatting happily.

It was an amazing day. The wives provided a special picnic lunch in honor of the men. Bill and I sat in the shade eating the delicious food and getting acquainted with the islanders. As I answered questions about ourselves, I realized that we were regarded as an oddity. The unasked, but obvious, question on everyone's mind was: Why would an American family want to settle on a little island off the coast of Australia?

I answered the unasked question. "We came here because we wanted our children to know what real life is about. In the States children are given everything, with no responsibilities attached. They spend a lot of time inside watching TV. They're missing the wonderful world outside. We chose Australia because Bill was here during the war. He liked the space and the freedom."

They nodded politely. Although it seemed to make sense, the idea of trading a bustling, prosperous America for a quiet Australian island was hard for them to comprehend.

By late afternoon the remaining food had been given away. The fish caught for the contest had been measured and prizes awarded. "I didn't win," Rusty grinned, packing up his rod, "but I came pretty close."

Mickey was thrilled when it was announced that he was First Place Winner of the Sand Garden Contest. "You always have done well at building," I congratulated him.

Making sure that the Moores were all accounted for, we boarded the homeward-bound ferry, a happy and contented bunch. "I think I'm going to like island living," I said. A chorus of voices echoed, "Me, too!"

When we docked at Russell, the Grahams offered to give us a ride home. "Are you going to the dance next Saturday?" Mrs. Graham asked as we chugged up and down the hills. "It will be held at the Parrish Hall. You're welcome to join us."

"Thank you," I said, smiling. "It sounds wonderful."

After we got the children settled, I told Bill about the dance. "It would be interesting," he mused, "I'd like to see what an Australian Saturday night dance is like."

The sky was pitch black that Saturday, but the air was fresh and crisp. The old 1929 blue Willes pickup truck we dubbed "Rackety Boom" had quit. It came with the farm, but didn't want to work after its last owner left. Walking was our only means of transportation. "The hall is a ten minute walk up and down hills, do you think you can make it?" Bill asked with concern.

I was seven months pregnant and, like most Americans, only accustomed to walking from the house to the car. But I answered confidently, "I'll be okay."

Picking our way by flashlight, Bill's ten minute walk took longer than expected. Finally, topping the last hill, we looked down to see bright lights streaming from the windows of the hall. Inside we were warmly welcomed.

Glancing around, I noticed that the dance was a family occasion and made a mental note to bring our children to the next dance. But for tonight, we were contented to be alone. We settled on one of the benches just as the lights flickered and went out.

"The generator," I heard someone say. Flashlights clicked on and several men went out to assess the problem. They came back shaking their heads, "It's a broken shaft," they announced to the shadowy figures behind the flashlight's glare.

"Fair dinkum," someone said. "We'll get out the Coleman lanterns." Flashlights moved into the kitchen area where rattling and clinking was followed by, "Jolly good! We've got it." Suddenly, a bright glow illuminated the room. The lanterns gave ample light to carry on with the festivities.

Music for the dance was provided by the islanders. I recognized Mrs. Schreiweis from Macleay at the piano. The elder Mr. Pointon, who was seventy-two, played the harmonica and violin. And sometimes, alternated on the drums with Mr. Wilson.

The dances, "Boston Two Step," "Pride of Erin" and "Gypsy Tap", were danced with partners in patterns similar to our Virginia Reel. The best dancers began, and the rest followed in a circle. All ages joined in—even the littlies. They were considered partners and were waltzed around happily in someone's arms.

During the evening, I watched babies being passed around to be cuddled and admired. When they fell asleep, they were comfortably bedded down under the benches, where nothing seemed to disturb them. One mother explained, "We put them under the benches so they won't get stepped on."

Since we didn't know the dances, we were contented to sit on a bench and chat with new friends. But my feet weren't content. They kept tapping to the music. I knew that somehow we would have to learn these dances. They involved the whole family and seemed to be so much fun.

At the end of the evening, Mrs. Graham announced that she would be teaching the dances to teenagers. "Would the teens mind if we joined the class?" I asked, well aware of the gap between teens and adults, that was so evident in the States.

"Not at all," she said, "we often have adults."

I smiled at Bill, "We're in!" I said, "This is going to be great."

Chapter Four

It's a Different World

IN THE NAVY, BILL DEVELOPED THE ability to jump to attention from a sound sleep—and still does. He's an early morning person. I'm just the opposite—a late night person. At 5:30 a.m., the sound of Bill's axe announced a new day. I moaned. I did not want to be awake. I did not want to get up. I pleaded with myself, "Just a few more minutes to stretch." And then I heard the kookaburras greeting the morning. Their raucous laughter chided me for missing any part of a new day on Russell Island. I crawled out of bed and went to see what Bill was doing.

Sleepily I stood at the top of the stairs watching him chop kindling for the stove. The first faint tinge of red had spread across a sky still bright with stars. The sun, planning its day, watched the moon march toward the horizon. Morning dew on the chicken wire sparkled like diamonds. I took a deep breath, "All's well with the world," I sighed.

Things were falling into place. Rusty and Skippy helped Bill with the outside chores, while Mickey gave me a hand in the house. Tia was in charge of the chickens. Blending the American word "chicken" with the Australian word "chook" she dubbed them "chookens."

The chookens were named by color groups, the "Browns," the "Whites" and the "Speckles." When Tia was still new at the job, Shirley Brown, her favorite chicken, died. We were all very sad and shared her disappointment. "Perhaps the other hens will lay some eggs and you'll have baby chookens," I encouraged, trying to cheer her up. Days passed but there were no eggs.

Talking over the fence, with our neighbor, Jack Wynn, I mentioned that our chickens weren't laying eggs. "Nest boxes," he advised, "they need a place to lay the eggs."

When I told Bill, he said, "We can fix that. I'll put some wooden boxes on a shelf in the hen house and line them with straw."

The hens were delighted with their cozy nests and Tia was delighted with the results. "Look!" she cried, running up from the hen house one day, "Look, an egg!" We all gathered around to admire our first egg.

"Finally, we've produced something on our farm!" Bill declared. Next we made an egg-production chart. It was watched closely and anxiously by all hands, as though we were personally responsible for laying the eggs. Eventually, the thrill wore off and the chickens were left in peace to enjoy their nests.

Benji was another pet. He came with the farm. A cute, little gray puppy with black spots. Skippy fell in love with him on our first visit. When Mr. Towers, the previous owner, said, "I'll leave him here for you," Skippy was thrilled.

Benji had already been trained to come to the foot of the stairs for food, but not up the stairs into the house. As he grew, he proved to be a wonderful pet and a faithful friend. The children always called Benji before they went up into the fields. He was a great snake dog. "He can smell a death adder or black snake and break its neck before we even know it's there," Rusty boasted. Since Australia has an abundance of snakes, Benji was a great comfort to have around.

Mickey came home one day with a calico cat. "It's a stray," he said, "I named it Tiggie. Can I keep it?" Seeing my frown, as a thumbs-down vote, he pressed on. "People say you need a cat on a farm to catch mice. This one's a male cat."

The gender did it. He had won his case. I added one condition: "Cats love to live outside, and that's where it must stay." By the time we discovered it wasn't a male it was too late. In no time, we had a whole family of mice catchers.

With the pet issue settled I realized that every farmer's wife has a kitchen garden. So I planted one. The puppy thought it was a place to dig. The cats thought it was a litter box. The chickens got out of their pen and clucked, "Dinner time! It's dinner time!"

The children ran through the garden chasing the puppy, the cat and the chickens! Surveying the trampled carrots and squashed lettuce I mumbled, "Now, what does the farmer's wife do? I know!" I answered myself, "I'll call the farmer."

Farmer Bill said, "We can fix that." He dug deep holes and planted four eight-foot high corner posts. Next he connected them with six-foot high chicken wire. He added a nice tall gate with a latch further up than any child could reach. It looked very impressive—as though we were planning to raise a gaggle of geese or something equally important. "No, it's only the kitchen garden," I told our curious neighbors.

Later, we were given a dozen baby ducks. "They're so cute," Pam cooed holding a little ball of yellow fluff. The little balls of fluff quickly grew in to chunky white Muskovy's, with red wattles. When Curtis heard about the Muskovys he warned, "Those critters multiply rapidly." He was right. They did.

"What can we do with them?" I asked Bill. "They're running all over."

"We'll," he paused, thinking, "You're not using the garden enclosure right now, are you?"

"No. Not since you started planting veggies in the rows with the other crops. Why? Do you want it for the ducks?"

"It would help," he said with relief. The fenced enclosure turned out to be ideal.

We were never short of roast duck dinners. Their eggs made tasty bread pudding when the hens were on vacation. But around our house, animals and fowls never seemed to stay put for long. These were no exception. We were always chasing escapees. At first it was not a big problem, but as the flock increased it was. They began to take over the farm. We gave away as many as we could and took the eggs out of their nests so they wouldn't hatch any more broods. Finally, with relief, the ducks were gone but vegetables became a problem.

"Did you bring some veggies down for dinner?" I would ask Bill when he came home from the fields.

"Sorry, I forgot," he'd apologize.

"That's okay, I'll send the boys up to get some."

How much better it would be, I reasoned, to have veggies close at hand, with no more flashlight-forays to pick them while we waited for dinner. The empty pen told me it was time to start another kitchen garden. Already fertilized by the ducks, the garden was a great success. Good healthy plants that needed no poison sprays. At last, we had achieved something that was less comedy and more substance.

Taking care of business on the island was easy. The general store, the post office, the bank, and the telephone exchange were all in the same building with two entrances. We went into the post office to pick up our mail from Mr. Wilson. Then, going around the building to the store entrance, we were served again by the smiling Mr. Wilson. He had turned around from the postal counter to become the store clerk.

The bank and the telephone switchboard were also at the post office. When we dialed a number from home, we were sometimes informed that the person we wanted to reach was out on his farm, off to the mainland, or visiting Mr. and Mrs. So-and-So. Another service provided by the smiling Mr. Wilson. "I like this system," I told Bill.

"That's good," he replied, "just remember, in Australia every local call costs five cents."

"No matter how long I talk?"

"That's right," he said. Considering that a loaf of bread was twenty-five cents, we did not make many phone calls.

Food shopping was more difficult. The little store carried only the barest of necessities. Theoretically, I could put in an order one day and it would be relayed to a store on the mainland and sent over the following day. In practice, it might arrive days later, or weeks—or maybe never. It was the "maybe never's" that were difficult. With a limited amount of money to spend, I debated on whether to reorder and possibly get twice as much, or just wait and hope.

One day I was sharing my frustration with Curtis, who was helping Bill fix a cranky tractor. Bending over the tractor with a wrench in his hand, he asked, "Have you tried Q.P.S.?"

"What's Q.P.S.?" I wanted to know.

"Queensland Pastoral Supplies is a catalog warehouse in Brisbane. You can place an order and they'll send it over on the mail boat. They have all kinds of food supplies."

Q.P.S. could have been called S.O.S. as far as we were concerned. Each month we ordered by catalog, a la Sears and Roebuck. When the order arrived it was like Christmas; a two-pound jar of real, unprocessed peanut butter, a twenty-eight-pound tin of "full-cream" powdered milk, a ten-pound round of Swiss cheese, whole wheat flour, tins of butter and "first break" cereal designed by God. Thankfully food processing was not a big business in Australia.

"First break cereal," Tia read on the package. "What's that?"

"That's wheat that has been cracked only once instead of all ground up and cooked like corn flakes in the States."

"Oh," she said, "will I like it?"

"Of course," I assured her.

Produce was a different story. We had a bountiful supply. Neighbors shared from their surplus or traded with us. On any particular day we might have on hand ten kinds of vegetables from avocados to sweet potatoes, and six kinds of fruit. Bananas and paw paw were always available.

"Farm life has great advantages," I told Bill, as I peeled a banana snack.

We ordered our meats and two-pound loaves of whole-wheat bread at the store. The meat and the unsliced, newspaper-wrapped bread, arrived the following morning on the mail boat. Like most islanders Bill gleaned the latest news while he waited for the boat to arrive. "More news than the morning paper," he declared, dumping our supplies on the table.

One day after finishing my chores I wandered outside and asked Bill, "What can I do to help?" I was eight months pregnant and needed a job without too much bending or lifting.

Bill thought a bit, "The bananas need trashing. But I don't know if you should do that kind of work."

"Trashing bananas! What do you mean?"

Bill explained that banana trees produce new leaves as the old ones die. "If the stiff, dry leaves remain on the tree, they scratch the tender bananas when the wind blows. And who wants to buy a scratched banana?"

"Well, how do you do it then?"

"You use the machete," he said. I knew what a machete was. It was a jungle knife about two feet long. Bill had one when we lived on Guam.

"Lift the dead leaf," he instructed, "and chop it off with a quick upward stroke close to the stalk."

He handed me the machete and I went to work. The banana grove was peaceful and quiet. It was a lovely day to be outside. "Lift and chop," I repeated to myself as I swung the machete upward. I don't know how it happened. One never does. It just happened. I saw the blood before I felt the pain. I had sliced into my left thumb, lifting a generous amount of skin, like peeling a potato.

Quickly, I ran back to the house and wrapped a clean cloth around my thumb, and went to find Bill. I knew he would be upset and blame himself, but I couldn't bandage my thumb without help. He was working on the tractor. When he saw the damaged thumb he was shocked, "How did you do that?" he frowned.

"I don't know," I mumbled, "but I need your help to bandage it."

"Come on," he said guiding me into the house like a child. "We'll need something to make a splint to keep your thumb from bending or it will never heal."

I fished a popsicle stick out of the craft box. "Will this do?" Nodding, Bill doused the cut with antiseptic while I gritted my teeth. Between the two of us we managed to bind it up. Just as we finished Mickey came in with a question, "Dad, do you know what to do with a pig?"

"What pig?"

"Skippy found a pig." Mickey had a habit of starting any discussion in the middle, or well towards the end. It takes endless questions to determine what he's talking about. Patiently we learned that Mr. Capper's pig was down the road. "It's injured," he said. This would have been complicated information, if we didn't already know that a pack of dogs had killed ten of Mr. Capper's piglets. Skippy had found one of the two piglets that were still missing.

After more questions we learned that Skippy had discovered the piglet in the brush and it was bleeding. Having no stomach for more blood, I let Bill handle the situation. He found Skippy, cleaned up the pig and put it back in its pen. Mr. Capper was not at home.

It's a Different World

I was in the kitchen trying to prepare dinner with my useless thumb when I heard a commotion. "What now!" I muttered and hurried outside. I saw Bill and one of Mr. Capper's boys crouched low, stalking up and down through the banana rows. Mr. Capper, dark-skinned, with shaggy white hair blowing in the wind, was following behind with a rifle in his hands. Shades of the old West—or a Ma Kettle movie! What was going on? Who were they after?

"Do you see them?" Mr. Capper cried out to his son. His son answered in an Australian accent so strong it sounded like a foreign tongue to me. But I understood enough to realize that they were hunting for the pig-killing dogs.

Just then Skippy riding bareback on our pony, Big Red, charged into the scene with a clatter of hooves. Hearing the commotion the girls ran up from feeding the chickens. "What's the matter?" they chorused. "What are they doing, Mommy?"

As I stared at the tableau in front of me, I mentally stepped back to include myself in the picture. Elbow bent for comfort I was holding up my throbbing thumb, still clutching the green beans I had been fixing for dinner. Incredible! The dogs were never found but forever after, Mr. Capper eyed every dog with great suspicion—especially Skippy's dog.

Benji's pedigree was part Blue Queensland Cattle Dog. Queensland "Bluies" were prized possessions of cattle drovers. Bluies performed the jobs of many men. They knew the ways of the cattle they "worked." By the time Benji was full grown, he could hold his own against any dog on the island. Benji was not a pig-killer, but he sure could defend himself.

Chapter Five

Broken-Downsville

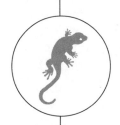

"Guess what, Mom," Rusty asked, munching on his morning snack while I worked in the kitchen.

"What?" I asked, pouring him a glass of milk.

"Did you know our tractor can bend in the middle?"

"No. Tractors don't bend in the middle, you're kidding."

Showing up for his treat, Mickey nodded, "This one does. It's a German Holder. It's a funny machine that was designed to bend in the middle when it turns corners. I don't like it. I call it the Green Beast. "

"It's not turning corners now," Bill said, appearing on the scene. "I can't get it to start. I think I'm beginning to understand why Mr. Tower's son left this farm."

"Oh, dear," I said. "What are you going to do?"

"Well, as soon as I finish my cookies and tea, I'll go talk to Mr. Russell. Curtis told me, he knows how to repair this kind of tractor."

Mr. Russell helped Bill fix the tractor. Bill gave him a days work in return. It wasn't long before another part broke down. This time Bill had to send to Germany for a replacement part. The tractor sat in sulky silence for three weeks, while we waited. No plowing, no crops.

Finally, the parts arrived. The tractor was happy again and spring plowing was well under way. We rejoiced—but not for long. We were eating breakfast one morning when the Graham boys ran into the yard out of breath. "Your tractor is burning!" Jimmy gasped. Bill ran out. They were right! He hastily scooped up dirt to smother the fire. Surveying the damage he realized that all the wires had burned and would have to be replaced.

"How long will it take?" I asked. I was hoping that we wouldn't have to send to Germany for more parts.

"I really don't know," he sighed, "I'll see what I can do."

This brought to a halt a whole lot of farm production—and house luxuries. Like wood for the kitchen stove. Although our wood supply was free, it had to be cut. When the boys couldn't find enough wood around the farm Bill checked at Poynton's saw mill to see what might be available.

"I've got these slabs," Mr. Poynton said nodding toward some outer bark cuts. "We trim these off before we slice the logs into boards. Carry away as many as you can use," he offered.

Some were as long as ten feet. Bill brought them home with the tractor and trailer. To cut them into stove-sized pieces, he attached a saw to the tractor power-take-off joint. With the tractor down for the count, he would have to saw by hand. A very difficult job. We reduced wood consumption considerably. "A farmer's life," I punned, "is a tough row to hoe."

A few days after the tractor broke down for the third time, Bill told me he was going to the mainland. "I've got some business to take care of," was his only explanation. That evening at dinner, he made an announcement. "I bought a tractor," he said.

"You what?" He hadn't even hinted at what he was going to do.

"Yes," he went on, "I went to Boonah. There's a place there that sells used equipment. I found a Fergerson Ford tractor that'll be just right." He turned to the boys with a grin, "This one's a big one. It was made in America and doesn't bend in the middle."

"Wow," Rusty said and whistled. "When do we get it?"

"It'll be sent over on the barge next week," he promised. The boys were thrilled. They chatted away about the great things they were going to do with a bigger, more powerful tractor. I heaved a sigh of relief, "Perhaps there's hope for us after all."

The next day sitting on the steps during our Saturday morning snack break, I contemplated the overgrown yard. "What can we do?" I asked Bill. "The yard is a mess. They say, snakes like to live in tall grass like this."

"Too right. We learned that at school," Mickey said. "And," he added, "just like everything else, the power mower that came with the this place only lasted one day. We should call this farm Broken-Downsville."

"Well," Tia joked, "the grass isn't broken. It keeps right on getting higher and higher." Without a word Bill retreated into the shed. We heard him digging into the dark corner full of junk. Finally, he emerged carrying an ancient eight-inch-blade push-mower.

"Here you are." he said triumphantly, "You boys can start mowing."

"Let me try!" Mickey volunteered, always ready to experiment with something new. Fifteen minutes later the mower had chewed up only one square yard of grass. "This is going to take forever," Mickey said wiping his sleeve across his forehead. Rusty and Skippy rose to the challenge but couldn't do any better. Finally, they all threatened to leave home and never come back.

Just then the boss appeared around the corner. "Hon," I called, "could you sharpen the blades on this thing? And maybe oil it." He did. It was still only an eight-inch cut but it took a lot less time and effort. Nevertheless, the boys prayed fervently that one day, God would magically drop a new, motorized grass cutter from the sky.

We planted beans and the mice ate the seeds. We planted peas and the irrigation failed. Could anything else break down? Yes. The boat. "What boat?" you ask. Well, while we were still in Brisbane we bought a twenty-foot launch with a cabin and an inboard motor. It was agreed that we could keep it at Breakfast Creek in Clayfield until we moved to the island.

When things settled down, Bill decided it was time to go to Brisbane to bring the boat over. "It will take me two hours to get to Clayfield," he explained the morning he left, "and another six hours to get home with the boat. I should be here by this afternoon," he assured me. Afternoon came—and went.

At dinnertime I told the children, "Dad's not home because he may have had trouble starting the boat." The boat had been sitting unused for a long time. Except for a trial run, Bill had never used it and wasn't familiar with the motor. As dark approached, I tried not to panic—or to let the kids know I was worried.

All evening I had one ear primed to catch his step on the stairs, but there was no sound. I settled the girls for the night, and went to talk to the boys who were finishing their homework. "Is Dad back?" Skippy asked.

"No, he's probably visiting someone in Clayfield. Of course, he can't call to let us know because the phone service is off for the night," I explained calmly. That satisfied them and they went to bed.

There was nothing else I could do, but try not to worry. I leaned back in my chair, closed my eyes and dozed off. Suddenly I woke. Something was wrong. Bill wasn't home! It was after midnight! Who could I call? The police? The Coast Guard? The Navy? Then I remembered that the phone service had shut down. I couldn't call anyone until it opened in the morning.

I was reminded of all the nights I had waited and worried when Bill was a Naval undercover agent in Japan. I knew Bill could take care of himself, but I wasn't sure about the boat, or the water. I prayed. God is so faithful and has always taken care of us. I spent the rest of the night trying to be calm. But I couldn't help wondering about things like, "How far will the insurance money go to feed and shelter six children? How could I possibly manage on my own?" The night seemed endless.

Early in the morning, as soon as the service went on, the phone rang. I sprang to answer it. "Is this Mrs. Moore?" an unfamiliar voice asked.

"Yes." I whispered, clutching the phone cord. I held it so tightly, I could feel the pain of my nails digging into my palm. I waited.

"Your husband has sent a message," the voice said. "His boat battery died while he was still on the Brisbane River. An early morning fisherman found him stranded. He wants you to know he'll be home as soon as he can."

The knot inside my stomach began to unwind. I eased my grip on the phone cord, thanked him and hung up. Everything was going to be all right. I took a deep breath. I felt like collapsing into a pile of rubble, but I called the children instead. "Dad's on his way home. He'll be here when you get back from school," I assured them. I busied myself getting the children ready for school. Then to keep occupied, while I waited for my sailor to return from the sea, I prepared a hearty meal.

Weary and blotched with mosquito bites, he climbed the stairs to a warm welcome. I quickly heaped his plate and sat down to hear what had happened.

Between bites he explained, "The motor wouldn't start so I found someone who started it with their battery. I figured the battery would be charged by the time I got home. I had just gotten to the river when the motor quit again. By then it was dark. All night, I could see the lights of cars driving on the shore. But I couldn't yell loud enough for anyone to hear me. I was marooned—right there in the bay. It was so frustrating.

"The mosquitoes drove me crazy. I spent the whole night fighting them off. This morning, just as it was getting light, a fishing boat came near enough to hear me shout. After the fellow started my motor with his battery, I gave him our phone number. He told me he would get a message to you. Did he ring?"

"Someone rang for him," I explained. "What did you do then?"

"I went back to Brisbane to get the battery charged before I started out across the bay again..." His last words trailed off, his head began to nod.

I leaned over. "Let me get you to bed before you fall asleep." I took his arm to help him up. Steering him toward the bedroom, I whispered softly, "Thank God you're home safe."

The Seagull

Chapter Six

An Australian Baby

I PEERED AT THE CLOCK. IT WAS JUST before midnight, July 15th. I was having strong indications that the baby was getting ready to be born. I lay there thinking... all the other children had been born on Tuesdays or Wednesdays. The midnight clock had just ushered in Wednesday. I hesitated between going over to the mainland on a false alarm—or the probability of delivering the baby on my own. Drowsily I rehearsed what I knew about the birthing process; scissors, hot water, tie off the placenta....

I must have dozed off. A sharp pain jolted me awake at four o'clock. I nudged Bill, "Hon, I think I had better go to the hospital. Would you see about the boat?" Bill sprang up, wide awake. Quickly, he dressed and was off.

Knowing that foot power would be faster than the tractor, he ran to the other end of the island to wake Mr. Vellensworth. They drove back to the post office to the only phone available during the night. Mr. Vellensworth rang Jack Noyes on Lamb Island. "We're going to need the launch to take Mrs. Moore to the mainland," he explained. Next, he called Brisbane to arrange for an ambulance to meet me at Redland Bay.

I was ready and waiting, when Bill came rushing back to the house. "Everything's set," he said quickly, "Jack Noyes is on his way, and the ambulance will be waiting for you when you get there. I'm going to run down to Mr. Hamlin's to see if he'll drive you to the jetty." I nodded in relief and he was off down the steps taking two at a time.

Beginning to feel like a community project, I placed my suitcase beside the door and sat down to wait. When I heard Mr. Hamlin's car chugging up the hill I went out to meet them. Bill took my suitcase, settled me in the car and we were off.

We arrived at the jetty just as the boat pulled in to the dock. Carefully, I was handed aboard. After making sure that I was comfortable, Bill gave me a hug and waved goodbye as the boat moved off. I waved back, smiling with a confidence I didn't feel. This was the first birth I would face completely on my own. I sat on the deck watching the night fold into day. It was brisk and cold. I smiled to myself as I thought, *This will be a winter baby, born in July. How odd.*

I sensed that Jack Noyes was a little nervous. Wondering if he had ever delivered a baby, I went up front to put him at ease. "Everything is fine," I assured him.

"Jolly good," he smiled. "Won't be long now." Much to his relief—and mine, the ambulance was waiting at the jetty. The friendly driver was a welcomed sight. "Owyerdoin?" he asked, helping me into the front seat.

An Australian Baby

"Jolly good," I said using an Australian phrase. "Ahh," I sighed, settling down for the hour long trip to the hospital, "this is the most comfortable vehicle I've traveled in since we landed in Australia."

To my surprise, the baby did not arrive on Wednesday. The doctor wanted to send me home. "Please don't," I said anxiously. The thought of going back to the island for a repeat of last night was more than I could cope with.

The nurse interceded, "Mrs. Moore came from the islands," she explained.

"Oh," the doctor said. I held my breath as he paused. "Righto, she can stay."

I spent the next two days walking up and down the hospital corridors to encourage the baby to get on with it. Not to be rushed, our son arrived on Saturday. He weighed in as the family heavyweight at seven pounds, nine ounces. The birth process was relaxed and informal. Much more natural than the operating-room style of American deliveries. As soon as I could get to a phone, I called Bill to tell him the good news, "It's a boy! Tell the children they have a baby brother."

"What's his name?" I could hear the girls asking.

"David Allen."

"No, you can't!" they exclaimed. "There are two boys who live down by the jetty. One is David and the other is Allen, and they're mean to us."

"That's right." I heard their brothers agreeing in the background. "It's the Murray boys."

To name a baby is hard enough. But when you've already used up three boy-name combinations, it's difficult. I thought a bit. He's the only one in our family *not* born on Tuesday or Wednesday. He weighs more than any of the others did at birth. His hair is much darker... He tops the list in many ways. That's it!

"Why don't we just call him Topper for now?" I told Bill. "Everyone will see how special he is when I bring him home next week."

The hospital food was terrible, coddled eggs and other soft mushy things that I can't stand. I was slowly starving but always hoping the next meal would offer something I could stomach. That night at dinner time, I smelled the roast beef and potatoes all the way down the hall. "Thank goodness," I breathed, "I'll be able to eat." The nurse put down my tray and went on with her rounds. I lifted the cover and looked—coddled eggs! I collapsed on the foot of the bed and began to cry.

Someone must have alerted the nurse. Suddenly, a voice above me said "I'm Nurse Fountain, is anything wrong?" She was kindly sympathetic when I told her I was starving and wouldn't be able to nurse my baby. She glanced at the food on the tray and looked at me. "Everybody in Australia loves coddled eggs," she said in surprise.

"Not me," I wept, "I can't stand mushy foods." Growing up I was known as a picky eater and I hadn't changed.

"Well," she explained carefully, "the doctor put you on a soft diet because of a complication in delivery and the number of stitches. He didn't want any strain on the affected area."

I looked at her, teary eyed and whimpered, "But I'm hungry."

"I think I can fix that," she said, and sailed off down the hall. Fifteen anxious minutes later, Nurse Fountain made a triumphant entry. She was carrying a plate of what looked like fried chicken. "I hope you like rabbit." she said with enthusiasm.

An Australian Baby

It looked good, and smelled good. I was desperate, but I had never eaten rabbit before. Seeing the doubtful look on my face, Nurse Fountain smiled. "It tastes just like chicken, you'll like it," she said, with such confidence I didn't dare argue. Nurse Fountain was easy to love. I did like it. At least it was firm and crisp.

By the time my stay was over, I had developed a bit of Australian accent to take home with the baby. Before we left the hospital, Topper had been officially named Brian Timothy Moore.

The ambulance took us back to Redland Bay to catch the ferry. When the driver realized that the launch wouldn't be in for four hours, he was concerned about leaving us at the jetty. With a phone call, he arranged for me to stay at the ambulance manager's home, near by. The manager's wife was very kind. She insisted that I take a nap while I was waiting. It was just what I needed to be ready for homecoming.

When we arrived at Russell Island, Bill was waiting with the Graham's car. "The Grahams wanted to be sure that you had a comfortable ride home," he explained, as he tucked us in. "With the westerlies blowing you don't need to be in an open tractor trailer." The "westerlies" were not good. They brought cold, winter weather and covered everything with gritty dust. July—yes, summer—no. It was winter.

When the children heard us coming they poured out of the house to welcome Mom and their new baby brother. They had spent the morning cleaning house and dressing themselves up for the grand occasion. Inside, the dining room table was decorated with fresh flowers and lace table cloth. It was set with the best china and ready for dinner.

Despite the cold, the girls had put on summer dresses. Their hair was stiff with dirt from the westerlies. To a practical eye, they were a pitiful sight with cold legs and cold noses. But to this mother's loving eyes, they were beautiful.

"Can I see the baby? Can I see the baby?" Jackie cried, reaching for my little bundle.

"Let's go inside first so he won't get cold."

In the house, everyone took turns holding Topper and wondering who he looked like. We finally decided that he looked a little bit like everyone, but mostly like Jackie. Except that his hair was brown and her's was red.

"Where is he going to sleep?" Pam asked. She was right, where was he going to sleep? The expected household shipment had not arrived. It was a disappointment, but "making do" had become second nature to us.

"I have an idea," I said. "If you will help me, we can make a special baby bed. Pam, you and Jackie get the baby sheets and blankets..." They were off before I finished talking.

"Mickey, you and Skippy can start putting the food on the table. Rusty, you hold the baby. Dad, would you get the bottom bureau drawer for us? Tia," I said, taking her hand, "let's go fix a place for Topper to sleep. We can call it a bassinet even though it isn't. Can't we?" She glanced at me with puzzled look, wondering what Mom was going to do next.

Quickly, I folded a soft blanket to fit the bottom of the drawer and covered it with the baby sheets and blanket. Rusty gently placed Topper in his little bed and tucked him in. The drawer, set on top of the bureau, had been transformed into a beautiful bassinet. A new era for the Moore family had begun.

Chapter Seven

Unforgettable Events

"Mom," Mickey asked, "why don't we go to church any more?"

"Because," I explained, "we live on an island and there is no church. That's why we have our own Sunday service right here."

"Well, what does everybody else do?

"I'm not sure Mickey, but I'll ask Mrs. Graham. We're going there for a Sing tonight.

That evening, Mrs. Graham told me that a priest had been coming over once a month, but he had been transferred. "Now there is a new one," she said. "Perhaps he doesn't know about us yet."

"That's probably the case," Mr. Graham said, "I'll ring up the new priest and let him know we're here." He went on to explain, "in the mainland schools, Thursday afternoons are designated for clergy to teach religion classes. Each child goes to the class of his particular faith."

"That's a great way to reinforce children's beliefs," I agreed. "It lets them know that faith is more than a Sunday thing."

Finally, arrangements were made for Father Brosslen to visit the island on the second Friday of each month. He came on the noon-ferry and left on the five o'clock after-school boat. During that time, he taught the children at school, and finished the day with a mass for the island's half dozen Catholic families.

At first, services were held at the Grahams' home. Later our young neighbor, Sergio, let us use his brand new house which wasn't far from the school. Sergio had built it for his parents who were immigrating from Yugoslavia. When they arrived in Australia, they decided to settle on the mainland instead of coming to the island. "The house is for sale," Sergio explained, "but it's empty and you can use it until it's sold."

We thanked him and began to make plans for a church. The Grahams allowed the kids to bring benches from the school. We made an altar by propping our card table up on gallon-sized paint cans. One for each table leg. We draped the table with a white sheet and decorated it with candles and flowers. "It looks like a proper church," Bill declared, viewing our work.

Each month Bill drove Father Brosslen up from the jetty and brought him home to eat lunch with us. He was a huge man in both girth and height. During his first visit, Bill mentioned that that we were just learning to farm. He told Bill he had been brought up on a farm out West. After lunch, he pushed back his chair and stood up, "Let's go have a look at your farm," he said. It became a regular event. Each visit he and Bill walked the fields together, discussing planting problems and farm management.

"He gave me a lot of helpful information," Bill told me after he drove him back to the jetty.

"Wonderful," I said, "we can never get too much of that. Did you ask him about baptizing Topper?"

"Yes, he told me next month would be fine."

At dinnertime I announced the coming event. "Now that we have a church, we can plan a christening party for Topper."

"Can we make some cookies?" Tia asked.

"And cakes, too," Skippy suggested.

"I can pick some flowers," Pam offered, "Jackie will help me, won't you Jackie?"

Jackie wasn't quite sure of what was going on, but sensed the excitement. She nodded with a grin and started for the door, "I can do flowers," she piped.

"Not yet," her daddy said, putting her back in her chair.

"Mom," Mickey suggested, "we could take the other folding table to use for refreshments."

"Don't forget to invite all the church people," Rusty reminded me.

When the big day arrived, Bill and I, with the help of Pam and Jackie, set up the altar. After naps, while Father Brosslen was teaching at school, we arranged the refreshments. The table and altar were decorated with flowers gathered by Pam and Jackie.

After the service, Topper, dressed in his little white suit and behaving himself very well, was baptized Brian Timothy Moore. The celebration was brief but lovely. Too soon, it was time to leave for the ferry. The Grahams offered to take the benches back to the school. Bill drove Father

Brosslen and the people from Macleay down to the jetty. The children and I began to clean up and gather things to take home.

Wrapping Topper in a blanket for the ride home, I pronounced solemnly, "You are now officially Brian Timothy Moore." As I laid him in his carriage, I told him that he had a big brother, William Raymond Moore III.

"That's right," Rusty said folding up the card table.

"And another brother," Mickey said, leaning over the carriage, "Michael James Moore."

Skippy jumped up on a chair. Swinging a cake knife in the air he proclaimed, "And another brother who is Richard Dale Moore." Hopping down, he peered into the carriage. "They couldn't figure out what to call me when I was born, either," he confided to Topper. "That's why they call me Skippy."

Tia, nudging him aside, smiled sweetly at her baby brother, "I am Teresa Louise Moore," she said primly, introducing herself with a courtesy. "Come on" she turned to Pam, "it's your turn. Tell Topper who you are."

"He knows who I am," Pam said, unimpressed with the theatrics.

Mickey scooped her up and held her over the carriage, "I present to you Pamela Marie Moore," he announced, as she squirmed to get down.

Tia tugged at Mickey's sleeve. "Do Jackie now," she said. "Jackie can't say her whole name."

"Come on, Jackie," he said picking her up. "See your brother, Brian Timothy Moore?"

"That's Topper," she said giggling.

"And you're Jacqueline Ann Moore," he said tossing her in the air.

It was my turn. "Do I need to tell Topper who I am?" I asked.

"Oh, Mom," they laughed, "you're silly."

"We had better get along then," I reminded them. "Dad will be home for dinner soon."

The following week, Nurse Fountain, my hospital friend of the fried rabbit, called to ask if she could come to visit us. I was delighted for an opportunity to introduce her to my family. Nurse Fountain was an immediate hit with Pam. Indeed, her caring, friendly nature captivated young and old.

We had just finished lunch, when Jack Wynn, from the farm up on the hill, came to the door. Before I could say, "G'day" he blurted out, "I just wanted to tell you there's a fire up at my place." He quickly explained that he had been burning a log so the smoke would drive the mosquitoes away from his horses. Wind blown sparks had ignited the grass.

"The fire is headed toward my house," he said, anxiously looking up the hill, "I need some help to get it under control."

Bill jumped up, grabbed his hat off the peg by the door and ran down the steps. The island was very dry. Fires were a big concern. When Bill didn't come back, Nurse Fountain declared, "They may need more help. I reckon I'll go up, too." She was an Australian who understood how quickly fire could spread.

"We'll go with you," the boys offered, trailing along behind.

I was washing dishes when Mickey ran back up the steps. "I need some matches," he puffed.

"Matches! for what!"

"Nurse Fountain says we have to start a back-burn."

"Fair enough," I said handing him the matches. "You

be careful!" I reminded him as he ran down the steps. Pam, Jackie and Topper were having naps. I decided it was safe to put Tia in charge. I followed Mickey up the hill to see what was going on.

The fire was spreading rapidly. I joined the others working feverishly to get it under control. We pounded it out with burlap bags and raked debris off the road to keep it from jumping towards our house. I sent one of the boys to tell Mr. Vellensworth at the store to spread the alarm.

Within minutes several men arrived and set to work. No longer needed, I decided it was time for me go home and rest. On the way down, I passed Jack Wynn. He was calmly wetting the burning grass close to his house, using a two gallon watering can with a sprinkler-head. *I wonder if he knows what he's doing* I thought.

Later, carrying cool drinks up for the firefighters. I found them sitting comfortably in the shade at the edge of the woods. They were spinning yarns as they watched the trees burst into flames. Australians can be very relaxed and practical about fires. As I poured their drinks one of the helpers declared, "Fair dinkum, we've done all we can."

Surveying the damage, I noticed that Jack Wynn had extinguished at least fifty yards of burning grass with his watering can and bucket. It seemed silly to me at the time, but it saved his house.

On the way to the jetty to catch the afternoon boat, Nurse Fountain couldn't say enough about the wonderful time she had spent with us. Actually, how often does one get to fight fire on an afternoon visit? The traditional tea and crumpets pale in comparison. When the Moores do things, they do them up right!

Chapter Eight

The Shipment Arrives

Topper was almost six weeks old when Bill came rushing home with the mail. "Our household shipment will be here tomorrow," he shouted.

"Oh no, we're just getting used to a new baby, and now we'll have complete chaos again."

Scanning the letter, he noted, "They're supposed to deliver six crates. They must be pretty big crates to hold all our stuff."

"Where will we put it all?" I moaned.

"Somewhere, I guess," was his less than helpful answer.

Mentally trying to place furniture I hadn't seen for over a year, I decided that everyone was in the wrong room. We spent the evening shifting beds, trunks and children. Finally satisfied, we fell into bed almost too excited to sleep.

The next morning two big trucks rolled

up from the jetty. They held six overseas crates, each one the size of a small room. As soon as they left, Bill pried open one that was full of boxes. We started unpacking. By the end of the next day, we had every inch of space on the porch, and the living room, piled with boxes.

It was like Christmas—every day. The children were all wound up. "I found my soldier set," Skippy exclaimed, waving a box of little soldiers.

"Mom!" Mickey stood in the door with a big box, "Can I open this one? I think my drawing set is in it."

"Where are all my dolls?" Tia cried, pawing through another box.

"Hon," Bill stood in the doorway holding two dinette chairs, "Where do you want to put these and the table that goes with them?"

Before things got out of hand, I called a family conference. Everyone gathered in the living room. "What's wrong?" Rusty asked, "Daddy said you wanted to see us." They were never sure about family conferences. Had they done something wrong, or was Mom going to outline a new policy?

"Nothing's wrong," I said, seeing their anxious faces. "Actually, everything is great. Are you happy to have our shipment here?"

"Yes!" they shouted in chorus.

"So am I. As a matter of fact I'd like to open every box right now, but there's just one problem."

"I knew it," Rusty sighed, flopping down on a chair.

"The problem is space," I explained. "We've been opening boxes willy-nilly and once they're opened we have to find places to put whatever is in them. Most of it gets packed into another box. Doesn't that seem kind of silly?" Relaxed, they giggled. "So, unless we have to look for something special, we'll only open one box at a time, and everyone will have a turn to choose a box."

"Can I have first turn?" Skippy asked.

"Well, we had better let Dad go first, 'cause he's the oldest. Then we'll work down the list. I'll be last, because I have to choose for Topper."

Fortunately, Mickey, had a gift for finding spaces and arranging things. He was a great help in working through the piles of stuff. Two months later we still had fifteen boxes to open.

"There's no room to unpack anything else," I told Bill. "Where did we get all these things?"

"I understand," he agreed with a shrug. "We do have a lot of things, and without electric power and water pressure some are useless. It would take a huge generator to provide enough electricity. What can we do with the Amana freezer, the automatic washing machine, and the radios?"

"We can put the freezer in the corner of the den and use it as storage. And, you never know," I said dreamily, "one day, we may have electricity from the mainland to operate all these now-useless things."

"There's always hope," Bill said, "but what about the children's stuff? It's scattered everywhere."

"Well," I suggested, "Perhaps, it's time to start a Penalty Box. That should make the kids feel at home."

"Of course," Bill said, "we used to collect coats, hats, toys and other abandon stuff."

"Yes, we kept them in a special box in the hall closet. The children had to redeemed them with a penny or a job."

"You're right," he agreed, "A Penalty Box would be the best sign that this is really home."

"Righto, good idea. Tomorrow I'm taking Topper over to the mainland for his six-week check-up. You can get the Penalty Box set up while I'm gone." I looked at him, smiling sweetly, "It's your turn to announce some bad news."

Bill grinned and changed the subject, "How are you going to manage Topper? He's too small for the walker, and the pram is too big to take with you. It's a long day to be carrying a baby around. An hour by ferry to Redland Bay, an hour by bus to Brisbane, and five hours in the city."

"Hi Mom, hi Dad," Mickey, home from school, entered the conversation. He looked at me, "Did I hear you say you're going to Brisbane?"

"Yes, I'm taking Topper over for his check-up. Would you like to go along, to help me carry him?"

"Sure, I can put Topper on my back in the Japanese carrier. I just found it in one of the boxes."

"That would be great. In Japan, you used to carry Pam on your back all the time, even for bike rides."

A "carrier" was used by Japanese mothers who took their babies everywhere. Made of a rectangle of cloth, lined and padded, it had two long straps on the top. They were passed over the shoulders, crossed in front, secured through loops on the bottom, and tied across the stomach. The carrier held the baby snugly against it's mother's back. Our carrier was made of black velvet cloth, with a pretty embroidered design on it.

The trip to town was a long tiring day but we had lots of fun. When we reached the city, Mickey put Topper on his back. I adjusted the straps and tied them across Mickey's stomach. Turning him around, I made sure Topper was snug with just his tiny head and toes sticking out.

Babies in back-carriers were not a common sight in Brisbane. We caused quite a stir, walking along the street. People passed by, noticed the baby on Mickey's back, and turned to stare with a what-in-the-world-is-going-on look. I smiled to assure them that the baby was perfectly all right.

We took a tram to the hospital for Topper's appointment. After his exam the doctor nodded and smiled, "He's doing very well," he announced. Great news for a mother's ears.

Back in the city Mickey and I celebrated with lunch and a double decker ice cream cone. "Boy, this is good!" Mickey said, lapping the drips running down the side of the cone. "Wish we could buy ice cream cones on the island."

"Perhaps, one day, we will," I said wistfully.

Chapter Nine

The Saga of Smokey and Big Red

FOR YEARS WE HAD PROMISED THE boys a pony. As soon as we decided to buy the farm, and well before we moved, they reminded us of our promise. Checking ads in the Brisbane paper, Bill and the boys had started their search. After their third try, they came home in high spirits.

"You want to see our ponies, Mom? I'll get the girls and we can all go."

"Skippy! wait a minute." He turned around. "Did you say ponies?"

"Fair dinkum, we've got two," Mickey said following Skippy into the room.

Coming through the door, Bill was quick to pass the buck, "They talked me into it," he said throwing up his hands.

"Mom, you should see them!" Rusty exclaimed, following his dad, "One is a big red pony and the other one is a dapple gray. You have to go see them."

Rounding up the girls, we had climbed into the van to inspect our latest acquisitions. By the time we got there, the kids had agreed to name the biggest one Big Red and christened the dapple gray Smokey.

When we reached the pasture, Jackie tried to climb up the fence, "I want to ride the pony," she piped.

"Not this time," Dad had explained, "I'm making arrangements for them to board here, until we move to the island."

That had been weeks ago. We had been so busy with other things, the ponies had been forgotten. Until Rusty reminded us one morning at breakfast.

"I guess we could manage them, now that we're settled," his dad told him. "The next time I go to town, I'll arrange for them to be sent over on the barge."

A few weeks later, Bill went down to the jetty to get the ponies. They were led off the barge wearing their saddles and gear. Bill tied them to the back of the tractor, and walked them home. When I heard the tractor drive into the yard, I rushed out to welcome the ponies. Big Red, more horse than pony, was friendly and calm. Smokey, much smaller, was nervous and jittery. "Why is Smokey so restless?" I asked Bill,

"I don't know," he shrugged. "The fellow, who runs the barge, told me that they had been tethered at Redland Bay all night."

"Do you think he needs to go for a ride?" I wondered. "I really don't know much about horses, but I would like a little run if I had been tethered all night." Bill agreed. He tied Big Red to the fence post where he could feed on the grass. Patting Smokey to calm him down, he put his foot in the stirrup and threw his other leg up over the saddle. Whoosh! In a flash Bill was flat on his back and Smokey was gone.

Quickly Bill untied Big Red and rode after the pony. Hours passed. *Bill is probably showing the ponies to the neighbors,* I rationalized. It was soon dark and no sight of Bill, or the ponies. I began to worry in earnest. The phone service had shut down for the night. *What could I do?* I fretted. *It's time to organize a rescue party, but how?*

I was tottering on a fine line between anxious and frantic, when Bill and Big Red plodded into the yard. Stiffly, he slid to the ground. "I think I have the worst case of saddle sores in history," he groaned.

"What happened? Where's Smokey?"

"Smokey kept just ahead of me. As soon as Big Red got close, he would move on. I couldn't get near enough to grab his reins. Finally, I realized I was getting nowhere." He settled Big Red, and with a groan, lowered the saddle and hobbled into the house.

Smokey roamed loose for two days, saddle and all. Things looked very black. We were afraid he would send us to the poorhouse by destroying someone's crops. "Perhaps," I suggested, "the next time you find Smokey, if you turn around and head home, he might follow Big Red, instead of the other way around."

Early the next morning, they went out again. Bill and Mickey walked, Rusty and Skippy rode on Big Red. I stayed at home pacing the floor. Hours later the phone rang. A voice I didn't recognize said, "I have a boy here with a cut leg. It's bleeding, so I have him sitting in the bath tub. Could you send someone to pick him up?"

I knew it had to be Skippy. I explained about the horses and that we had no means of transportation. The lady assured me, "There is no one at this end to bring him home just now, but not to worry."

Not to worry! I couldn't stop worrying any more than I could keep the sun from going down. And that's what the sun was doing. It was getting dark. "Where are my boys? Where's Bill?" Just then, I heard a motor coming up the road. I ran out, in time to see Rusty climb down from the rear-end platform of Mr. Wilson's tractor. Mickey followed, carrying a muddy saddle.

I suddenly realized it was Rusty who had been bleeding in the bath tub. Calm on the outside—but screaming on the inside, I helped him into the house to look at the damage. Thankfully, the cut wasn't as bad as I had imagined. With relief I realized it wouldn't require stitches.

While I cleaned and bandaged the wound, Rusty told me what had happened. "We were chasing Smokey when the saddle strap broke. I landed in the swamp and got cut by a piece of glass."

"You're going to be fine," I assured him. Then, holding my breath I asked, Where's Skippy?"

"He's still out there on Big Red, somewhere."

"Where's Dad?" I asked Mickey.

"I don't know. I told Dad I would stay with Rusty. When Mrs. Wilson saw Rusty limping she told us to come in."

I had no idea what the island was like beyond our boundaries. With so much to do in getting our house settled there had been no time to explore. My imagination was running wild. There could be lions, tigers, bears, deadly snakes—and it was almost dark!

Finally, I heard voices outside. Rushing to the landing, I looked down to see Skippy coming into the yard with his dad. The inside of me quietly collapsed into a heap of rubble. The outside smiled, "Are you all right? Where's the pony?"

"He's okay," Skippy said hugging Benji, who had rushed out to greet him. I looked at Benji's tail wagging happily and thought, *If I had a tail it would be wagging too.*

"Smokey is in Orme's paddock," Bill explained climbing the steps. "The Ormes have the only fenced paddock around. I finally got Smokey to follow Big Red. We left both of them there for the night." I knew right then, that I never would have succeeded as a pioneer's wife. All of this was too much. But the saga doesn't end there.

After we brought Smokey home, we tethered the ponies out in the fields during the day and brought them in at night. Smokey still refused to let anyone on his back. It wasn't long before he ran off again.

For several hours, Bill and the boys tried to catch him. It was dinner time. The chores were waiting. We needed wood for the stove to cook dinner, and to heat water for baths. Everyone was tired, hungry and dirty. Tempers were high. Bill sent for Lorraine Russell. She was a nineteen-year-old who had a reputation for handling horses, and wanted one of her own. "You catch Smokey," Bill promised, "and he's yours!"

With the help of Big Red, she finally got Smokey into Orme's paddock. The next day she brought him back to the farm. "Just until I can get my parent's permission to keep him," she explained. A week later, we realized that Lorraine's mother and father were the only people on the island who did not know that Lorraine was the owner of a pony.

Bill decided to make an enclosure for the ponies until Lorraine was ready to take Smokey home. It became a priority project. He collected posts and wire from the no-longer-necessary outer boundary fences. Working together, he and the boys fenced in a good sized paddock just below the house.

At last, Smokey and Big Red could run free. It was a joy to watch them playing tag, thrilled with their new quarters. The next night the game of tag became serious with Big Red gnashing his teeth and jabbing at Smokey. I went down to the fence and scolded Big Red. He stopped to listen and then settled down. When I told Bill how mean Big Red had gotten, he grinned, "He was probably letting Smokey know who's going to be boss of the new territory."

Even though we kept them in fresh fodder they began to yearn for the nicer things of life, like paw paw trees, sugar cane and other people's crops. Leaning over the fence they ate everything they could reach.

One morning we woke up to find Big Red in the chicken yard. Another time, they both escaped to roll in the pumpkin patch. They sampled Jack Wynn's sweet potatoes and grazed on his pea vines before we caught them. Jack Wynn had two big plow horses. "They never run off," I complained to Bill. "Why can't our horses behave like them?"

We spent a lot of time hand-feeding Smokey hoping to win his confidence. Gradually, he would ease up to the fence for food and sometimes let us pat him. Lorraine often came to take him for walks. One day he let her brush him down. But, he would not allow her to get on his back.

In the meantime, Skippy and Big Red got along very well. Bareback, with pounding hoof beats, they would charge into the yard. All I could do was close my eyes, take a deep breath and come up smiling. I could teach Skippy to be careful, but I refused to teach him to be afraid.

Two-year-old Jackie could handle Big Red better than I. One day he was wandering around the yard with a dangling rein. I tried to take the rein to lead him back to the paddock. He knew how scared I was of this huge beast. He jerked his head, every time I reached for the rein.

Jackie was standing nearby watching the show. Before I made a complete fool of myself in front of my wee daughter, I did the only sensible thing, "Jackie, catch Big Red and take him into the paddock, please." Pint sized Jackie walked over to that giant critter, grabbed his rein, and with a tug said, "Come on Big Red." And off he went as docile as a lamb.

Rusty was the only one who ever got on Smokey's back. It was a victory that lasted a matter of seconds. I didn't realize what was going on in the paddock until I heard the children yelling, "Rusty's hurt, Rusty's hurt!"

"He's laying on the ground!" Mickey shouted.

Running to the scene, Bill picked him up and carried him inside. He was holding his arm just above the elbow, "I think my arm is broken," he moaned.

"Broken bones... broken bones..." I muttered, as my brain searched through the volumes of information stored there. One thing I knew, Rusty needed to see a doctor. "Hon, you'll have to take him over to the mainland. Please ring for a boat."

"Righto, I'll make arrangements and get cleaned up."

"Broken bones... broken bones... I know! The Boy Scout Manual." I had seen it just the other day in one of the crates we were unpacking. I hunted through a pile of books. It wasn't there. Another pile. No, not there either. Another pile of books, and finally—the Boy Scout Manual! "Broken bones... broken bones..." I intoned as I leafed through the index. "Ah! here it is."

Following the pictorial directions I tied a sling around Rusty's neck to hold the arm in place. Then, I tied what they called a binder around his chest to hold his arm close to his body. I gave him an aspirin for pain, whispered a prayer and called to his dad, "He's ready!"

It would be a long boat trip and a long ambulance ride, before he could be taken care of properly. I prayed that all would go well. Thankfully, in a large family, there is never time to dwell on "maybe's". Chores needed to be done. Children needed to be fed, bathed and put to bed.

It was dark by the time I heard the truck drive back into the yard. I rushed out to the landing. As they came up the steps, Bill made his report. "He saw two doctors, and was x-rayed twice. The doctor said his upper arm has a slight break, but not enough to warrant a cast."

"Yeah," Rusty said, "I was sent home just the way I left. Only, I have a new sling around my neck and a new binder around my chest. Just like the Boy Scout book said."

"Thank God," I rejoiced. "Come on, I kept your dinner warm." Sitting with them while they ate, I vowed to keep that Boy Scout Manual in a very safe place.

For months we tried to tame Smokey by keeping him in the paddock and hand-feeding him. Although he came to us for food, and allowed Lorraine to brush him down, he was as jumpy as ever. No one seemed to have an answer for this strange behavior.

After a year of trying, Bill decided to sell the horses and buy a cow. Lorraine was working on the mainland and the boys were busy with school and farm work. "The boys won't miss the ponies, they've found other interests," he told me.

"If that's the case," I said, "I agree. The milk from a cow would be much better for the whole family."

Arrangements were made with their former owner to exchange Smokey and Big Red for a milk cow. The owner agreed to meet the barge and pick them up at Redland Bay. The cow would be sent over later.

On the next barge-day, Bill tied Smokey and Big Red to the back of the tractor, walking them the mile down to the jetty to meet the barge. "You won't believe this," he said when he came home.

"Believe what?" I asked.

He looked at me and shook his head in wonder, "The barge skipper climbed up on Smokey and rode him right on to the barge without any trouble at all."

"That is hard to believe," I gasped. I was stunned.

Chapter Ten

Thoughts from the Farmer's Wife

SITTING ON THE BACK STEPS, WATCHING the magpies perch on the clothesline, I thought about the past few months. We had coped with a new baby, stowed away our shipment, and even acted as firefighters. Except for crisis points, life was peaceful and quiet. Maybe too quiet.

Electricity was the big difference. I missed having lights at the touch of a switch, a stove available when I wanted it, and a washer that actually did the washing and wringing by itself. At one time, I thought of writing a book, "Life With Seven Children and no Automatics." Then I realized, it would probably be deadly dull, because most of my time was spent putting clothes on the line, and food on the table. Of course, putting food on the table wasn't as easy as it sounds. We worked from scratch.

One day, Bill came up the steps and handed me what looked like a football. "Jack Wynn sent you a sweet potato." He dropped it on the table and quickly left.

It was different from any sweet potato I had ever seen. This one was reddish on the outside and white on the inside. I tried to peel it. I couldn't. It was too big to hang on to. I tried to cut it into manageable pieces. The dinner hour was getting close and I was frustrated. Bill passed through the house as I hacked away. "What are you doing?" he asked, as he breezed by.

"Getting dinner," I said, through clenched teeth. "Are these sweet potatoes always this big?"

"I don't think so," he said, as he hurried down the steps.

The little interruption was enough to calm me down. "I know what I'll do," I announced to the empty kitchen. Under the house was a good sized chopping block, with an axe embedded in it ready to use. I took the monstrous potato down stairs and dispatched it into dinner size pieces, with a few swift strokes of the axe.

Mickey came by just as I gathered up the pieces. What are you doing, Mom?" he asked with a quizzical look. When I explained, he said, "Jolly good." He thought Mom was pretty clever. The chopping block became a well-used solution for oversized potatoes.

Almost as funny, was my first experience at hanging clothes on the line, er… clothes hoist. The hoist was a great invention made of a four-inch metal pipe cemented firmly into the ground. It had four five-foot arms that stuck out like a compass, north, south east and west. Wire lines were strung in between. There was a crank handle on the main post—for folding the arms, I supposed.

The first time I saw one in Australia, I thought it was pretty neat. But I had to jump to hang the clothes. The lines were so high! How ridiculous I thought. Only a giant would want something like this.

Finally, I wondered if the crank handle had another purpose. I turned it a few times. My clothes rose high in the air and began spinning in the breeze. I cranked it the other way. My clothes stopped spinning, and descended to a level where I could harvest them like a bunch of bananas.

"That's the greatest invention I've ever seen," I told Bill at dinner. "The clothes spin around, dry quickly and are practically wrinkle free." Without saying anything he smiled his, I'm-glad-you're-happy smile.

Since it wasn't practical to run our generator all the time, we only used it during the day for laundry, ironing, and to operate Bill's tools. At night we turned it on for lights, sewing, records and radios. We had heard rumors of power lines being strung across Russell Island. They were needed to provide electricity for the mining industry on Stradbroke Island. In that case Russell would be in the loop. We would have electricity all day—every day! My heart raced at the thought. Will the rumors ever come true? I could only hope.

To keep our minds sharp, Bill and I studied French with the school teacher's family. On my own, I studied agriculture hoping to develop an organic farm. Bill kept me supplied with text books and magazines from the library. His Aunt Jac, who lived in Maine, sent books on farming by Rodale, Faulkner and Bromfield. She introduced me to environmental books like Carson's *Silent Spring*.

When we bought the farm, the only money crop growing was a few rows of sweet potatoes. Bill dug them by hand, the island way, prying them out of the earth with a tire iron. He washed them in a tub, bagged them in a burlap sack and took them to the jetty. There they were loaded onto the barge for Monday's market in Brisbane. "That seems like an awful lot of work for a few potatoes," I said.

Over hot cups of coffee we talked endlessly about improving our output. Enthusiastically we spent a whole morning measuring fields in the rain. At that time it was always raining. Our plans looked great, drawn up on paper. But then... Bill decided to do his farming with Jack Wynn.

Jack Wynn, an independent sixty-year-old bachelor, was still using horses to plow. He only planted ten rows at a time and seldom bothered to harvest them. Jack was in the process of building a house, but after five years, the islanders were making bets on whether it would ever be finished.

In the meantime he lived in a shack on the property. "You should see it," Bill said after a visit. "It has a dirt floor, with a narrow rut that leads to a mosquito netted bed. The only other furniture I saw, was a little homemade table, a chair and a small stove. All sharing space with a collection of junk. I guess that explains why Jack does his visiting down at the jetty, or at the store. He seems to be a very lonely man."

Bill thought working with Jack would be a good way to learn about farming. But he soon realized that Jack was still in the horse and buggy era. I gently reminded him, "That's all right for Jack, he doesn't have to feed a family; you do."

Poor Bill was torn between Jack and me for months. Jack would say, "Burn the hedge rows."

I would say, "Don't you dare. That's where the insect-eaters live." Bill knew Jack had been farming for thirty

Thoughts from the Farmer's Wife

years. He also knew that I had no farming credentials at all. But—he understood—he had to live with me.

Even so, being a farmer suited Bill. He loved what he was doing and worked from dawn to dark. After stopping for the day, he could be found stretched out on the floor, somewhere sound asleep. Just before ringing the dinner bell, I would tell the nearest child, "Go find Dad." No wonder he took naps, there was always something that needed to be done.

One morning, he and the girls came home from getting the mail. "I want some honey," Pam said, as Bill unloaded the tucker bag.

"Sorry, we don't have any honey. How about peanut butter and jam?"

"No," Jackie said, "Mr. Wilson said we have honey."

I looked at Bill. "Remember the hives," he said. "Mr. Wilson asked if we were enjoying the honey. I guess we'd better do something about the bees."

The farm came with two bee colonies in white hive boxes. They were out in the tall grass behind the generator shed. We cautioned the children not to go near the hives, especially Rusty, who is allergic to bee stings. With so much to learn, and do, we had forgotten about harvesting honey.

Beekeepers we are not; willing to try we are. Bill sent to the library for a book about beekeeping and tossed it into my lap. Curious Connie took the bait. I learned about wings, legs and stingers, but found almost nothing about the "how-to's" of actually harvesting honey. "The only thing I'm sure of," I told Bill, "is that beekeepers wear screen veils over their hats to prevent stings."

"That's not much to go on, but I'll try it anyway." He put on extra pants and a jacket. "Do you mind if I borrow the mosquito netting from Topper's carriage?"

"What for?" I asked.

"I'm going to put it over my hat." I watched as he arranged it over his hat and tucked it into his jacket.

"And, for extra protection, I'm going to use the mosquito netting from our bed." He put it over his head, gathered it up and strapped it around his waist. Covering his hands with gloves, he announced, "I'm ready to be a beekeeper."

He didn't fool the bees one bit. They knew he was no beekeeper! He managed to remove only one frame of honey before the bees got under the net. Yanking it off, he ran for the house with the bees in angry pursuit.

We got out the encyclopedia and looked up beekeeping. The next day he made a smudge pot, took a shower, put on clean clothes and covered his face with the small net. This time he was able to harvest the honey with only a couple of stings.

"Jolly good!" I said when I saw the frames full of honey. "Now what are we supposed to do?"

"Curtis told me to put the honeycombs into a burlap bag, hang it up and let the honey drip into a pan. He said to leave it for a few days until all the honey drips out. I'll rig it up now in the shower room."

A week later we had a bountiful supply of delicious honey. I poured it into jars while Bill cleaned up the frames and returned them to the hives. A few days later, we noticed the bees weren't buzzing around the hives any more.

Wondering what was wrong, Bill went to see Curtis. "Did you replace the wax?" Curtis asked. "Bees have to have wax to rebuild their combs."

"Encyclopedias are great for information," Bill said when he told me the bad news, "but they don't tell it all."

Later, the kids ordered a children's book on beekeeping from the extension library. It told us exactly what to do. Of course, it was too late—the bees were gone. But at least we knew where to look for information for beginners when we needed it.

Bees weren't the only buzzing insects we had to deal with. Mosquitoes were another challenge. "Somewhere," I told Bill, "there must be statistics, to show that Queensland has the biggest mosquito population in the world. Most of them probably live right here on our farm."

They had met us the day we arrived, buzzing to each other, "Fresh blood, city blood!" It had been a wet spring, perfect for mosquito breeding. All we could do was scratch. Fortunately, someone on the boat passed us a bottle of "Kodiak" mosquito repellent. "It's the best kind," they said. "You can buy it at the store on the island." We did. It was a blessing.

"I've got some good news," Bill said unloading the mail one day.

"Stop scratching," I told Jackie, "Come let me put something on your bites. What's the good news?" I asked over my shoulder.

"Mr. Vellensworth said that people living on the islands actually become immune to 'mozzie' bites."

"Jolly good! But how long does it take? Mosquitoes keep us inside the house as much as winter snows back home in Maine." All summer long, they covered our window screens whining and buzzing. I remembered Mr. Tower's pride when he mentioned the screens as a selling point for the farm. Many times, I blessed the person who had installed them.

We wore long pants in the fields to protect our legs, "They still bite when I bend over!" Mickey complained.

"There not biting me," Bill boasted.

"That's because you have drill work clothes on," I told him. Bill was wearing khaki pants and a shirt left over from his navy days. "Too right!" I exclaimed. "I know what we can do."

I ordered from Q.P.S. six sets of khaki work pants and shirts in Bill's size. We hung them on pegs near the kitchen door. Before going outside to work we put them on over our clothes. The boys and I folded over the front of our pants and used a big pin to reduce them to our size. We let the shirts hang outside for double protection when bending over. Like knights of old we had discovered that arrows—and mosquitoes—cannot penetrate layers of armor.

"Here's another good deal," Bill said. "We can make our own smudge pots. Curtis showed me how." He took an empty tin and attached a bit of wire for a handle. "Now," he said, "when we're ready, we just drop in a few burning sticks, and every once in a while, we drop in a handful of green grass."

"That's right," Mickey said, "The grass makes it smoke and the smoke keeps the mozzies away!"

Dressed in our "armor" and armed with smudge pots, I asked the kids, "Do you think knights of old had to cope with mosquitoes?"

"I guess," Skippy said.

"Maybe they used smudge pots, too," Tia suggested.

"I hope so," Mickey laughed. "Because they really work!"

Chapter Eleven

Changing Crops

EVEN WITH THE MOSQUITOES, THE ISLAND was beautiful. The weather was seldom too hot or too cold. The people were friendly, and there was never a dull moment. Before we left Perth, our friend, Mrs. Kiley had told us, "Queenslanders are the best in Australia. They're more friendly and have a sense of humor. If one loses one's sense of humor," she added sagely, "life isn't worth much."

Russell Island carried it a bit further. It was a place where your neighbor could be a titled Scotchman, or a widowed countess with a house full of precious antiques. A place where you work from dawn to dusk, making far less money than you ever dreamed—and finding it less important all the time.

Even though we started out as green as grass we were learning every day. One big lesson, was our two acres of bananas. "All you need is fertilizer," the farm agent told us, assessing our badly neglected trees. We invested time and money trimming the over-growth and spreading the magic fertilizer.

A few months later Bill asked if I would go check the grove with him. Biting into a ripe banana, I offered my opinion, "I don't think these bananas will ever take the market by storm. They're great eating but pretty scrawny."

"Your right," he agreed, "the Robinsons on Macleay send out ninety, sixty-pound bunches a week. We send out six, twenty-pound bunches. It's obvious we need to rethink our banana business."

"Why don't we just save enough banana trees for our own use?" I suggested. "That way we'll have acreage to plant with something else, and still have bunches to hang under the house for the kids. Bananas sure beat a lot of other snack foods." I broke off another ripe one and peeled it for Bill.

"Did you ever think you would have a banana plantation right in your own back yard?" Bill asked, biting into his banana with a satisfied look.

"Never in my wildest dreams," I laughed. "By the way what are you going to do about that field with the old tomato-stake wires. The one that's full of weeds?"

"I've asked the boys if they would tackle the job of winding the wire this Saturday. We can save the wire to be used later and clear the land for another crop."

Saturday morning, after I put Topper down for his nap, I went up to check on the boys. When I arrived on the scene they were thoroughly discouraged. The dead plants were dry, brittle, and over grown by a tangle of weeds. The reeler would unwind itself every time the boys let go of the handle to separate the weeds from the wire. I watched them work for a few minutes and asked, "Would it help if the reel didn't unwind?"

"Yes, Ma'am, but it does," Rusty groaned.

"Maybe I can fix it," I said, "I'll be right back." I ran down the hill to the house and found what I needed in my sewing closet. Quickly I made two loops of heavy elastic and went back. When I reached the field, I saw my workers stretched out on the grass contemplating the clouds.

"Why am I in such a rush?" I asked myself. They were obviously in no hurry for me to solve their problem. Without disturbing them, I attached the elastic loops to hold the reel. I called the workers to test my invention.

"It works," Mickey confirmed with a smile.

"Too right!" Rusty approved, raising his eyebrows in surprise.

"Now we have to go back to work," Skippy sighed, looking at the other side of the coin. It took a lot of effort but the field was finally cleared.

"Have you ever heard of passionfruit?" Bill asked one day as he took his work clothes off the peg and slipped them on."

"Only that they are about the size of a plum and have a lot of seeds," I answered. "Why do you ask?"

"See that field with tall grass?" he said, pointing up the hill.

"What does that have to do with passionfruit?"

"Well, that's our passionfruit crop."

"Passionfruit crop!" I echoed, "Looks like grass to me. Is that where you're going to plant the passionfruit?"

"No, the plants are already there. Mr. Towers said his son never got around to putting up the posts and stringing wire for them to grow on. You know—like grapes."

"Oh! What do we have to do?" I was hoping he would say plow them under and plant beans.

"Well, passionfruit is a good cash crop and these are already grafted. All we have to do is put in the posts, string wire and untangle the vines from the grass."

"Oh no!" I said, "Ten rows of grafted passionfruit on the ground, in weeds, waist high! The boys will have a fit. You've got to be kidding."

He wasn't. He put in posts, strung the wires, and tied up the vines. Sadly, not enough plants survived to produce a crop for market. Undaunted, we learned to make thirst-quenching passionfruit drinks and creamy passionfruit frostings. Tangy passionfruit ice cream was one of our all time favorites.

"I guess it was worth all the work," Mickey philosophized, scooping up a big spoonful of passionfruit ice cream.

Seeing us struggling with unproductive crops, Curtis advised us, "Plant green beans, they only take eight weeks to market."

"Plant green beans," Mr. Russell told Bill when he went down to the jetty to wait for the boat.

"You could plant green beans," Malcolm McInnes suggested as they waited for the mail to be sorted.

Bill remembered his ten rows of beans with Jack Wynn and decided to think big. He planted twenty five rows. All of us went out to "chip" the rows. Bill handed each of us a long handled tool with a flat, oval shaped blade on the end.

"What's this?" Mickey asked, "Aren't we supposed to use a hoe?"

"No," Bill said, "This is a chipper. It's easier to use." He demonstrated. "Slide it around the plant and the blade will cut off the weeds at the roots. Just be careful not to cut off the plant."

I picked up my chipper and looked down the row. "Wow," I said, "how long are these rows?" They aren't like any garden I've ever seen.

"Only about 160 feet," Bill answered as he started to chip. It was too late to back out now. I followed his lead. With five of us working it took all day to finish the field. Later we learned to "hill" the beans by pulling dirt up around the plants with a hoe.

Finally, after weeks of Saturday's spent weed chipping and hoeing, Bill called his crew together. "It's time to pick the beans," he announced. We donned our work clothes and headed for the fields, armed with smudge-pots.

"Somebody's already been picking the beans!" Mickey cried when he got close enough to see.

"Look at the tracks," Rusty said, bending down to examine the ground. "Wallabies! They've been keeping an eye on our beans. I've seen those miniature kangaroos hopping around our farm early in the mornings. I bet they feasted on our harvest before we were out of bed."

"At least they left some behind," Skippy observed, as he snapped off a bean to chew on. We left the boys to pick the rest of the beans and headed back to the house.

"What are we going to do now," I wailed. "Do you think we'll ever make any money on this farm?"

"Don't worry," Bill said, as we walked back down the hill, "my Navy retirement will keep us going until we get the hang of this. We certainly won't starve, with all the food possibilities we have around. And when the boys get through picking the beans, we'll have enough for ourselves and some to trade."

Down by the house I pointed to a vine trying to cover the lemon tree. "If our crops would grow as well as that choko vine, we'd be rich." Chokos are a pear-shaped vegetable covered with prickly spines. Light green in color they are difficult to peel but tasty as a vegetable. And great for "mock" apple pies when there were no real apples around.

Bill thought for a moment, "That would be a good crop for Rusty to work on, since we've decided to keep him home and let him go to school with the island kids."

Rusty, getting into the swing of being a farmer, was enthusiastic about the possibility of a cash crop. He cut the vine back and made a trellis for it to grow on. In no time it had little baby chokos. Their fast growth was great encouragement. He was thrilled when he sent his first harvest to market and received a check in the mail.

"Wouldn't it be wonderful if everything grew like chokos," I thought, as I went down to work in my kitchen garden. I had added manure and a generous amount of mulch to the plot to create healthy soil. I was hoping I could do away with poison sprays and artificial fertilizers. According to the American farm journals, they were both bad news.

I had just begun to plant a section when Bill came along. "You have so much manure and mulch on top of the ground, the seeds will never make it up to the light," he mumbled, as he disappeared around the shed. So much for my experiment! "He's probably right," I sighed. I stirred the manure and mulch into the ground and decided to wait a few days before planting.

About that time, someone told us sweet potatoes would be a good crop for us. "Just pick some tips and plant them," they said.

"What are tips?" I asked.

"Tips are ten-inch pieces of vine from a growing plant," Bill explained. "They root when you stick them into the ground. The vines spread out to keep the weeds down. The potatoes grow under ground and, unlike tomatoes, they don't rot. Best of all they don't need to be sprayed like tomatoes and beans. And, you can harvest them when your ready."

"Sounds like the perfect crop for us. Where do we get the tips?"

"Sergio said we could pick some from his sweet potatoes. He's worked out a new way to wash and bag potatoes, too."

Over at his farm, Sergio showed us how he washed potatoes. "I just spread them out on the grass and spray them with the irrigation hose, while I shift them around with my feet. Takes the dirt right off," he said smiling. "You can copy what I'm doing if you want to." We thanked him and began picking tips.

"I think I'm going to like this crop," I told Bill as we worked. "At least we won't have to do as much chipping."

Taking our tips back to the farm to plant, we made it a family affair. Topper slept in the shade in his carriage. The girls laid tips in the open furrows Bill had prepared with the tractor. The rest of us, crawling along on hands and knees, patted dirt around the tips to make them stand up. Every one was excited about the results. We didn't have to wait for seeds to sprout and the girls loved the fun of playing in the dirt.

Looking pretty dusty we walked back to Sergio's to pick more tips. Tom Hamlin came along in his car and offered us a ride. I glanced back at the kids walking behind us. They were more than dusty. "Thanks for the offer," I smiled, "but

I think we had better walk this time. We're all so dirty."

"Righto," he said and drove off.

"That was nice of him," I told Bill.

While we were working, the Routledges came across the road and invited us over for a cold drink. Afterwards, Curtis, his wife Daphne, and their children helped us pick more tips. "I'm sure they felt sorry for us," I told Bill later. "We've been trying so hard to be farmers with such comical results."

"You're right," he grinned. "Were probably the funniest act to ever hit Russell Island."

Straggling down to the house, hot and dusty, we felt as though we had reached a turning point. "You children have done a great day's work," Bill said, "Your mom and I are proud of you." Turning to me, he asked, "Tomorrow is Sunday, could we have a picnic to celebrate our new crop?"

"Jolly good!" I said, giving him a hug.

The day after our picnic we added another big event to our new direction. Mickey rushed up the steps after school. "What's the name of our place?" he asked, dropping his backpack. Sitting in my rocker feeding Topper I thought, *here we go again*. I answered his question with another, more obvious one.

"What do you mean?"

"Well, other people have names for their farms. This one should have a name, too," he said, reaching for Topper who was straining towards him.

"I've never heard anyone mention a name. I guess we'll have to make one up ourselves. How about Fiddler's Green?"

"What's that?" he asked, bouncing Topper on his knee.

"Do you remember when we crossed the equator and the 180th Meridian?"

"Yes, I do," he nodded.

"We had a lot fun with old legends like Davy Jones Locker and the Golden Dragon."

"I know," he said, more interested in playing with Topper than old legends.

"Well, there is an old legend that Fiddler's Green is the place where good sailors go. I just read about it in Dad's Navy magazine. And since we've found a place of peace and contentment right here I thought it would apply."

I reached into the magazine rack for the book, flipped the pages and began to read, "Just in case you didn't know it, calm weather and smooth seas are the result of the sweet songs of the women of Fiddler's Green, who sing to keep the waves in unison. Whenever they stop singing, the waves get restless and bad weather ensues."

"Is that why you sing so much?" Mickey looked at me.

I smiled at him. "Music is a blessing, it really does soothe people. It says so in the Bible. Goodness knows we all need to be soothed at times."

"I like Fiddler's Green," he said, taking a laughing Topper off to play.

Fiddler's Green

Chapter Twelve

Christmas Down Under

How odd to see people mopping their brows and exclaiming with cheer, "It's getting hot, Christmas is near!" In Australia there is no snow, no frosted noses, the poinsettias are not red, they're green and leafy—they blossom in June during winter.

I find myself thinking, "It's summer time. Why are they singing Christmas carols?" As the days heat up, thoughts of Christmas are hard to capture. Completely out of focus are bits of wrapping paper with smiling Santas and red-nosed reindeer.

Discussions of Christmas trees and gifts are glossed over quickly, in favor of final exams and summer vacations. Into this topsy-turvy world, trickle cards with reindeer, Christmas trees, and snow covered houses, to prod us back to reality. In Australia, there is no all-consuming focus on Christmas, it simply flows along with all the other events of summer.

Running up the stairs, Skippy interrupted my thoughts, "Can we go to School Break-Up?"

"What's that?" I asked setting out cookies and milk.

"That's when school is over." Mickey explained. "They have a big party down at the school."

"Too right!" Skippy said, reaching for a cookie, "Mr. Wilson says the men begin early in the morning by kindling a fire under a big drum of water."

"That's so they can make tea all day," Mickey said, "Can we go down and help? Tables have to be set up under the school where it's shady. Mrs. Wilson told us the ladies will be there making sandwiches and punch."

"They're going to have watermelons, too, and games." Tia added.

"And, guess what!" said wide-eyed, Pam. "Jimmy Graham told me they're sending ice cream over from the mainland!"

"Goodness, how are they going to keep it from melting?"

"I know!" Mickey volunteered, "Mr. Wilson told me. It will come over on the evening boat, in a special cold-pack with dry ice. The Farmers Market in Brisbane is sending us cases of peaches and plums, too."

Reaching for the last cookie Skippy remembered that the ladies of the island were making deserts for the event, "Could you make some cookies, Mom?" he mumbled with his mouth full.

School Break-Up Day was all they promised it would be. The program included every type of competition imaginable for children and adults. Piggy-back races, three-legged races, potato sack races, spoon races, and egg races. There were competitions in rod casting and broom throwing.

After lunch, the children entertained the grown-ups with skits and songs they had learned at school. As the day ended, each child received a small bag of candy, a bag of fruit, and a balloon. A special story-book gift, chosen by the child beforehand, was presented, as a reward for sports or academic achievements. I marveled at the simplicity, and the abundance. It was a family day such as we used to have in America many years ago.

Following Break-Up Day, we were invited to the usual Christmas parties. The "bring-a-plate" kind (cookies and sandwiches) or the "family-kind" where the men talk to men, women talk to women—and the American, Mrs. Moore, talks to everyone. I discuss crops with the men and food with the women.

One morning, in the middle of breakfast, the phone rang, "This is Mrs. Wilson," she said speaking rapidly, "Saturday is Christmas Tree Night, the event of the year. The children really look forward to it. It will be held at the Jacksonville Hall." While I was still translating her Australian accent into American English, she added, "Festivities begin at 8:00 p.m., we're hoping you can come." Promising we would, I thanked her for the invitation.

"Do you know where Jacksonville Hall is?" I asked Bill.

"Yes, It's about a mile and a half down the road, in the opposite direction from the jetty..." he paused, sorting out his information. "There used to be a big pineapple cannery and sawmill down there. It's mostly gone now, but the Bay View theater is still there. I think they have a sports ground, too. Why do you ask?"

"That's where they have Christmas Tree Night and we've been invited. All the school children will be going."

"But that's the day of Tia's birthday party," he reminded me.

"Well, it's too late to reschedule and too late to cancel. The boys have been talking about Christmas Tree Night for days. I didn't know it was a family affair."

"Everything on Russell Island is a family affair," he shrugged. "We'll just move the party along quickly. The kids will be so focused on tonight they won't mind."

He was right. Everyone was tense with excitement. As soon as the last guest departed we dressed the girls for the big occasion. The boys took them down to Jacksonville in time to see Father Christmas.

In the middle of a quick clean up we stopped and looked at each other… the silence was deafening. No squealing, giggling children. We could talk to each other without shouting. Breathing a sigh of relief we dressed quickly for the "biggest event of the year."

By the time we were ready it was fully dark. We coated ourselves with repellent and tucked Topper into his carriage under a mosquito net. Bill let me carry the lantern while he pushed the carriage. The road had deep sand in the valleys and round, slippery pebbles on the hills. "I'm glad we only have a mile and half to go," I said as I skidded on the red, volcanic pebbles, that were deposited on the island centuries ago.

Reaching the top of the highest hill, we could see the lights on the mainland. My heart skipped a beat. Electricity, street lights! They were so close… but so far away. "Anyway," I sighed, "it's comforting to know that the world is still out there."

The Hall was packed with people from all four islands. Tia rushed over to tell us about Father Christmas. "There were presents under the tree for everyone," she said. "Look at what I got!" She held up a doll and a book. I admired her gifts and asked where Pam and Jackie were. "Right there," she said pointing toward the center of the dance floor. There they sat, right at home with the other littlies, eating ice cream and playing with their new toys.

Soon after we arrived, the school children entertained us with songs and little dances, while Mrs. Graham played the piano. It was indeed the biggest event of the year and our very first island Christmas.

When the festivities were over we started home. I pushed the carriage, while Tia carried the lantern. Skippy pushed and pulled Jackie's stroller through the sand. Bill carried Pam. We slid on the stones and got bogged down in the sand, but finally arrived back home. Just as we reached the yard, Topper's carriage, built for cement sidewalks, fell apart. "Island sand is not the same as Maine snow," I observed, picking up the pieces.

Christmas Day arrived at 12:01 a.m.—just as it always does. Surrounded by unfinished gifts I looked at the clock, there was still so much to do! "I don't think we're going to get this done before dawn," Bill sighed sipping one more cup of coffee.

"I have an idea." I grabbed colored paper, pen and scissors. Cutting out small squares, I wrote, "To-be-assembled-later." We wearily wrapped up pieces of unfinished projects, attached the notes, and crawled into bed.

Skippy was up at three o'clock, doing his chores. He wasn't going to miss one precious moment of Christmas.

"Skippy," I moaned, "go back to bed. Christmas isn't official until six o'clock." You can fool some of the people some of the time, but not kids—not for very long anyway. By 5:30 a.m., we were all up, greeting the day with hot chocolate, cinnamon buns and a prayer of thanksgiving.

For weeks, the children had been pouring over craft books for gift ideas. Their presents were made out of construction paper, and whatever was available around the house. They were simple, but created with love. Dad made the girls a doll house, and for the boys, a small shelf to hang above their desks for school books. I had been busy sewing shirts and dresses. No one minded that some of them were just pieces with a promise.

The last gift was a big mysterious box. It looked impressive. Rusty, as the oldest, was designated to open this puzzling package. "Hurry," the kids urged, crowding around him.

"I am," he said peeling off layers of paper. "Just be patient."

"Who wrapped this one?" Skippy wanted to know, as the layers were peeled away. Finally, Rusty lifted the lid. "It's just a stupid ball of string," he said in disgust.

I couldn't stand the look of disappointment on their faces as Rusty stood there holding a ball of string. "Perhaps it's attached to something," I suggested innocently. Rusty tugged on the string. His face brightened. Everyone scrambled and shouted as they followed the string out the door, down the yard, around the shed, and there it was! A car! Mickey identified it right away, "A 1939 Oldsmobile!" he shouted.

After being without transportation for so many weeks, anything looked good to us. Bill had traded the old tractor Mickey had dubbed the "Green Beast" for the car. It was almost the newest car on the island! We celebrated by driving to Brown's pool at Canipa Passage for a picnic and swim.

"This is the only pool around," Bill said, as we unloaded things from the car to a picnic table. "That's right," Rusty added. Canipa is an inside passage from Brisbane to the Gold Coast. The Browns cater to the sailboat crowd."

Mickey set the picnic basket on the table, and we headed for the pool. "It's nice here," he said. "With the cabins and the pool, it makes a great stop off place for surf-boarders going to Surfers Paradise. I guess that's why they built it."

"I don't care why they built it," Tia said, poised to jump, "I'm just glad they did." A big splash followed her words. Thanks to the "Christmas car" our world had expanded—if only, for just a few miles.

Back home, we had an elegant candle-light dinner. For the first time since we had arrived in Australia, we used our china, crystal and silver. It was even cool enough to pretend it was a proper winter Christmas.

Chapter Thirteen

Stradbroke Adventures

STRADBROKE IS AN ISLAND ABOUT twenty miles long. It shelters our island from the ocean. At one time, Stradbroke served as a penal colony and was the home of several Aborigine tribes. It still boasts of wild cows, horses and kangaroos. A great attraction for hunters and adventurers—like my crew. They decided to explore the island during their summer vacation.

"It'll be a good camping trip for the boys," Bill said. "Mr. Orme told me he would row us over in his boat and drop us off."

"Row over to Stradbroke! Isn't that a long way to row?"

"No, it's only about a quarter of a mile. We'll take the camping gear in our backpacks. We can walk across the island to the ocean, and have some fun fishing, swimming, and maybe hunting. Depending on how it goes, we'll be back in two or three days," he assured me.

Finally it was arranged that Kenny Orme, Gary Wilson, Rusty, and Skippy would go on the trip with Bill. Mickey was to stay with us and make a trip later. We helped them load their gear in the car and waved goodbye, "Have a good time! We'll see you in a few days," we called as they drove off.

Two days later, Mr. Jackson's truck pulled into our yard. Curious, I looked out to see Bill and the boys climb down from the rear of the truck. They stashed their backpacks under the house and plodded wearily up the steps. "That was a quick trip," I said, "Did you have a good time? Can I get you something to eat?"

"We've already eaten," Skippy said, "do you have any cookies left?"

"Yeah!" Rusty perked up.

"I'll take a cup of coffee and some cookies," Bill sighed, leaning against the doorway.

"Sit down at the table and I'll have them ready in a jiffy." I could see that something was wrong. I put the coffee, milk and a plate of their favorite cookies on the table and sat down. "Tell me about your trip. Did you get across the channel all right?"

"Sure did." Bill said, "we crossed at the narrowest point. It didn't take long. As soon as we landed, we loaded our gear and started climbing up a steep hill on a winding trail. It was so narrow we had to walk single file. I was bringing up the rear, just behind Skippy, when suddenly he almost knocked me over jumping backwards..."

"Yeah," Skippy interrupted, "I yelled, 'snake!'"

Glancing at Skippy, Bill continued, "I looked where he

was pointing and saw a two-foot long death adder half buried in the sand. It was right in the middle of the path. The other boys had just stepped over it!"

"They did," Skippy said, round-eyed. "When Kenny heard me yell, he rushed back and killed the snake with his air rifle."

"When I realized three of the boys had already stepped over that snake," Bill said solemnly, "I was one worried man. This was not the camping trip I had expected. It didn't get any better either. At the foot of the hill we entered a swamp. No one had told me there was a swamp there. I found out later it's called Eighteen Mile Swamp. If it's that many miles long, I'm glad we were only going across. Even at that, it was about as bad as it gets. At times we were up to our waists in water or walking through swamp grass, jumping from tuft to tuft."

"Mom!" Skippy broke in, "I was walking right behind Rusty and all of a sudden he disappeared! All I could see were his hands holding on to his gun. It was his gun that kept him from sinking out of sight."

Rusty continued the story. "I jumped on a grass clump I thought was solid ground, but it was growing over a deep hole. The pressure of my weight made it cave in. Luckily, I was carrying my gun up in front of me across my chest. It was wider than the hole so it stopped me from going any deeper. No telling how far down I would have gone without that gun."

"Skippy and I pulled him out," Bill said. "Fortunately, we found a bit of solid ground to get organized again. We were all badly shaken. But, there we were, in the middle of the swamp with no place to go but forward."

Skippy picked up the story. "A few hours later, we came

to a place called Swan Bay. You should have been there, Mom. It was like a fairy-tale land! It had moss hanging down from trees and everything was reflected in the still water."

"We could see eagles watching us from their perches," Rusty added. "We watched a flock of white egrets feeding at the water's edge. And, I guess we startled some kangaroos because we heard them thumping through the bush."

"It was a beautiful place," Skippy sighed, "but eerie, like Never-Never land in the movies. One of the best parts of our whole trip."

"After a while," Bill broke in, "I held my hand up to quiet them down. When they all stopped talking we could hear the surf rolling in on the beach! We were so relieved we started to run. But just across a stretch of sand we found ourselves in another swamp."

"It was awful!" Rusty groaned, "the worst of the worst. Just when we thought we were out of that stuff!"

"Everyone was exhausted and smarting from the grass cuts," Bill frowned. "It looked as though we would never get free of that place. But we finally did. We left the swamp, climbed up the nearest dune and looked out on the ocean. 'We made it!!' the boys started yelling. For a while we just stood there breathing in the salty air. I looked at my watch. It had taken us four and a half hours to travel about five miles."

"Every one was so excited!" Rusty exclaimed. "We dropped our heavy backpacks and started hunting for a good camp site. We found a perfect one. It was between the sand dunes and the ocean. And right next to a steep red cliff to protect us from the wind."

"That ocean was the best sight I've ever seen," Skippy said laughing. "As soon as we finished setting up our tents we all ran for the water."

Bill smiled, remembering the sight of four boys dashing for the surf. "I figured the ocean's saltiness would probably be the best thing for the swamp grass cuts. I let them play while I gathered wood for the fire. They certainly had earned their play time. After a while I got hungry and called, 'Who wants to fish for dinner?' They all ran to get their fishing rods. In no time we had a fine catch of whiting sizzling over the fire. After we ate there was no argument about going to bed. No one was interested in staying up to tell campfire horror stories. We had had enough.

"The next morning I crawled out of our tent and went to check on the other boys. They were still asleep. But all around us, I noticed hoof prints in the sand. A herd of wild horses had checked out our tents during the night. Probably wondering about the intruders who had invaded their territory. Surprisingly, we had not heard a sound.

"Sitting around eating breakfast, I asked them what they wanted to do. Go back the way we came or walk up the beach to Dunwich and get the barge to Cleveland. 'Go to Dunwich!' was the unanimous decision. I told them it's a long walk."

"Not as long as the swamp," Skippy said.

His dad glanced at him and smiled. "We broke camp, shouldered our backpacks and headed up the sandy beach. We walked along between white dunes speckled with sea oats on one side, and the roaring surf on the other. It was a beach as beautiful as anything Hawaii has to offer."

"There were lots of shells and sea birds, too," Skippy volunteered.

"That's right," Rusty said, "When the world discovers the beach at Stradbroke, it will be standing room only."

"Too right!" Skippy agreed. "As it was, we were the only people there. We didn't see a soul on the fifteen mile walk to the road that goes across to Dunwich."

"The hike across the widest part of the island to Dunwich was twice the distance we crossed yesterday," Bill explained, "but no one cared. We all agreed that anything was better than Eighteen Mile Swamp."

"You bet!" said the boys, drifting off for baths and bed.

"Fair dinkum," Bill said when they were gone, "the boys were great. I'm proud of them. But that was one scary vacation."

"Just think," I poured another cup of coffee, "in a few weeks you can look forward to another exciting Stradbroke trip."

He grinned, "Somehow, I don't think Mickey will want to take our route. I suspect he'll plan something quite different."

He was right. Mickey's trip could have been called the "Bike-a-lot Vacation."

"Dad," he asked making plans. "When we go to Stradbroke can we take our bikes?"

"And Benji." Skippy added, thinking of the death adder in the swamp.

"You said I could take Harold Orme, too." Mickey reminded him.

"Well, if we're going to take four bikes and one dog I'll have to see about getting Mr. Jackson to ferry us to the mainland. Then we'll have to find a way, to get to Cleveland to take the barge to Dunwich."

Mickey's face lit up. "We can ride our bikes! It's only eight miles."

"And Benji can run." Skippy volunteered, catching

the excitement. "He's strong... and fast!"

"All right, but when we get to Dunwich, where do you want to camp?"

"Mr. Orme told me there are some little cabins at Amity Point. Could we stay in one of those?"

"How do you plan to get to Amity? It's at least five miles from Dunwich."

"By bike, of course." Mickey said. Skippy stood by, nodding in agreement.

"I'll check about renting a cabin. If I can arrange it, would you like to go next weekend."

"Sure!" Mickey said, turning toward Skippy, "Come on, lets get our things together."

"Okay, but I have to tell Benji first."

They spent the week making plans. One night at dinner, Mickey talked about biking to Lookout Point. "Can we do that, Dad?" he asked.

"Do you know how far that is? It's at least ten miles from Amity, up and down hills steeper than you've seen for a long time. They twist and turn all the way."

"I bet we could make it," Skippy said looking confidently at his brother.

Bill made arrangements for a rustic cabin with four bunks and a kitchenette. A little general store was within walking distance. Mickey's idea of a perfect vacation! A cabin *and* a store.

They stayed there for full three days and came home with lots of tales. "Every night, Harold and I caught enough fish for dinner," Mickey said proudly.

"We went swimming and did lots of bike riding," Skippy added.

"You should have seen the hill going up to Point Lookout!" Mickey exclaimed. "Sometimes we had to get off our bikes and walk, it was so steep. Going down the hill was tricky, too. We had to be careful not to skid off the trail."

Putting out cookies and milk, I asked Skippy, "How did Benji behave?"

Mickey answered for him, "Skippy worried about him all night."

"Well, I was afraid he would run off chasing something and get lost. But he was all right," Skippy grinned. He was the proud owner of a good dog.

"I'm glad you had a wonderful time and pleased that you got back on schedule. I didn't have to spend hours worrying about you. By the way, why did you bring your dishes back dirty?"

"We didn't have enough water to wash them," Mickey explained.

"Oh! really," I said in mock surprise, "whatever happened to the ocean?"

Chapter Fourteen

Smelling the Roses

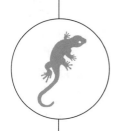

CHRISTMAS VACATION WAS OVER. THE children bubbled with excitement when we met for morning prayers and Bible reading. Today was the start of a new school year. During our first six months on the island Rusty had attended boarding school on the mainland. It seemed like a good idea at the time, but we soon realized, that home and family were even more important.

Dressed in his Cleveland High School uniform and carrying a suitcase full of books he was ready to catch the 7:00 a.m. school boat. He wouldn't returned until 5:30 that evening. A long day away, but there were no complaints. It was better than having him away for weeks.

The other children had time for morning chores before their short walk to school. With their chores finished, one by one they called, "Good bye Mom, God bless you," as they skipped down the stairs. Clad in their Russell Island school uniforms and hats, they carried their books in their back packs. I stood on the landing and gazed with approval as they started off. Tia wore a kelly-green belted dress and natural straw hat with green trim. The boys had kelly-green shirts with gray shorts and felt hats. No neckties for boys—or girls. Shoes were considered an option, so we settled on white socks and tennis shoes.

The start of the school year meant new studies for the kids and new chores for Mom. I inherited Rusty's choko crop and Skippy's dog—at least Benji was supposed to be Skippy's dog. His tail wags him from side to side when Skip returns from school, but Bill is his best friend. Benji goes off with anyone who is bound for adventure, but he doesn't always wait for them to come home. Benji belongs to Benji, but he and I have our own special bond.

I give him sympathy when he shows up wounded and feed him cereal sandwiches for breakfast. While he takes the children to school, I put the leftover breakfast porridge between two slices of whole wheat bread. As soon as he gets back, he comes to the bottom of the stairs for his treat. When I start down the steps, his tail wags and his eyes smile. He tentatively puts a paw on the first step, but knowing his boundaries, he goes no farther. He stretches his neck out as far as he can to close the gap. Accepting his gift, he holds it gently between his jaws, and trots off to enjoy it in the shade of the willow tree.

As I sat on the steps watching him enjoy his meal, I thought of the past six months of pandemonium. Finally, we had reached a plateau. A time to stop and smell the roses. "*Here we are*," I thought, "*just two hours from the capital of Queensland, living the sort of life people only dream about."* The island was so quiet I could hear surf breaking on the shores of Stradbroke five miles away.

"What are you smiling about?" Bill asked joining me on the steps.

"I was thinking about our being able to swim in the ocean six months of the year. In groups of course, with an eye out for sharks. Or being able to juggle work around to suit any occasion."

"That's what you call good living," Bill agreed. "Especially when you have neighbors who are friendly and helpful. They always welcome me with a cup of tea when I drop in for a bit of advice."

I nodded, "Even when we're working, it's fun because we're together and everyone pitches in. I've gotten to like digging in the warm earth…"

"Look!" Bill pointed to a flock of rose-crested cockatoos. He called to Pam and Jackie, "Come down in the yard and see the white cockatoos!" Screaming loudly, the flock swooped overhead and landed in the eucalyptus tree.

"They may be noisy but they sure are beautiful."

"Mmm," Bill agreed. "And so were the green "budgies" we saw fluttering in the bushes last week. I guess that's what makes farming fun. Imagine, in the States, budgerigars would be caged pets."

Jackie had climbed up on her daddy's lap. "I like the kukaburras, they go haha, haha, hahaha," she yelled getting louder with each "haha."

"They really do laugh," Pam chimed in, "but they're awfully loud." She held her hands over her ears to make her point as she ran back down the steps. Bill and I sat quietly for a while. It was so peaceful, but hard to stay still for long.

I suddenly remembered the Christmas gifts that were "to-be-assembled" later. "Time to finish last year's business," I sighed, stretching. "I think I'll start by painting the shelves and the doll house while Topper's taking his nap."

"Let me know when the paint is dry," Bill called over his shoulder as he headed for the fields. "I'd like to put up the boys' shelves before they get home."

I chose several cans of paint and began the process of blending just the right color. Finally satisfied, I painted the boys' shelves and rinsed out the brush. Changing colors, I started on the doll house. As I dabbed paint around the windows, I chuckled. Imagine the look on people's faces if I told them I painted a whole house in one day. *Oh, well,* I laughed at myself. *Can I help it if my imagination has a funny bone?*

"If the week continues this well," I told Bill at lunch, "I'll have the girls' dresses, Topper's suit, and the dollhouse curtains finished before we start planting."

"That won't be long," he said, "I want to put in some sweet potatoes on Saturday. I'll pick as many tips as I can while you finish the other things."

I shook my head, "It's hard to think of planting crops in January. Back in the States we'd be wearing winter clothes and shoveling snow."

"Too right," he agreed.

Saturday morning, we donned our work clothes and set out for the fields. We carried fertilizer and bundles of tips. Working by hand, and hoe, it took us a full day to plant four rows. Walking back to the house exhausted, I complained, "Those rows are as long as two tennis courts. There must be a better way to do this. Surely we can figure something out."

Smelling the Roses

During the week Bill, Rusty and I put our heads together. "This is what we need to do," I said. "We need the plow to open the row. Then, we must find a way to put in fertilizer and cover it over while still leaving grooves for the tips."

Bill thought for a minute, "Well, if I attach the plow to the front of the tractor to open the row, and the scuffler to the back of the tractor to close it, we'll have grooves for the tips. But what about the fertilizer?"

"There must be a way to put it in before we close the row," I pondered.

"We could try a hopper," Rusty suggested.

"Jolly good!" I exclaimed. "We could use one of the twenty-eight-gallon tins that powdered milk comes in. Attach a burlap funnel," I mused, "weight it with a large metal washer and control it with a rope."

"Righto!" Rusty shouted enthusiastically. "Someone can sit on the front of the scuffler to control the fertilizer before it closes the row. How's that sound, Dad?"

Bill nodded in approval, "I see the possibilities. Let's experiment. I'll rig the tractor while you collect the materials we'll need." After a few adjustments in the experimental stage we were able to plant fifty rows in one day! The kids followed the tractor laying tips in the rows. The boys and I crawled along covering part of the tips. Bill followed us with a hoe to stand the tips up.

After lunch, Rusty developed another great innovation. Instead of crawling on his hands and knees, he started to dance. "Rusty!" his father called from the next row. "Stop playing, we need to get this planting done."

"Wait a minute," I cautioned, "he may have something. What are you doing Rusty?"

"I step on the end of the tip to stand it up, shuffle dirt over it from each side and finish with a step to press it down. Step, shuffle, shuffle, step."

"It works!" Mickey exclaimed, balancing on one foot.

I walked back along the row, "Let me try it. Now, how did you do that?" I watched him for a moment and tried a few practice steps. I like almost any kind of dancing. "It does work," I called to Bill.

"Well, okay," he said, after scrutinizing the results with a critical eye. Trying a few rows on his own, he declared with a smile, "The Moores have revolutionized the sweet potato business on Russell Island."

"That's what you can do with American resourcefulness and ingenuity." Mickey said proudly. We all cheered, "Hurrah!"

Sometimes, though, when the day grows long, I take off a glove to wipe a weary hand across my brow. Looking down at my engagement diamond sparkling in the sun I ask myself, "What am I doing here? Why am I crawling around in this dirt?" But that's only when I'm tired. The rest of the time, I know what I'm doing here. Enjoying life. Work is vital part of life's equation. My goal for the future? Grow what can be harvested by reaching up rather than bending down. Like passionfruit or avocados... a call from Tia broke in on my daydream.

"Mamma, Mamma, Topper's awake!" she called from the house. She's my alert sounder when Topper's eating alarm goes off. I made a beeline for the house. Slipping out of my work clothes, I quickly washed my hands and lifted Topper from his crib. Our sturdy little Australian was almost a year old and as happy as a song. Unless he was hungry—then he loudly let us know he needed attention.

"When is Topper going to talk?" Jackie asked, leaning on the arm of my rocking chair as I fed him.

"We can't be sure," I said, "but I know what he would say if he could."

"What would he say?" curious Pam inquired, sitting on the floor playing with her dolls.

"He would say something like this... 'I have a wonderful life with people who love me, play with me, carry me around, and take me for stroller rides.' That's what he would tell us."

Jackie giggled. "What else would he say?" Pam wanted to know.

"Well, I bet he would say... 'Tia feeds me breakfast and takes me for walks. Pam and Jackie play with me every day.'"

"Yes, we do," they cried in unison. "We give him our toys, too," Jackie added.

"What else?" Pam moved closer.

"I think he would tell us... 'When Mickey takes care of me I sit on his shoulders, bang on his head, and pull on his hair. But, he doesn't mind at all.'"

The girls laughed. I went on... "'Sometimes he puts me on his back like a Japanese baby and takes me for a ride on his bike. When I love him, I lean my face against his and make soft noises. That's how I love everybody in this house. Mom says I'm the sweetest baby in the whole world.'"

"Don't you agree?" I asked the girls as they took turns hugging their baby brother.

We cannot know what tomorrow will bring, or how the roses will smell, but for now, the roses smell sweet.

Chapter Fifteen

The Way Things Are

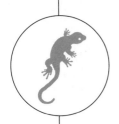

STRETCHING OUT THE KINKS, I LAY IN BED preparing for a new day ...Remember to mend Rusty's pants, read the farm bulletins, decide on lunch. Hypatia will be over to visit on the afternoon boat. It's the 3th of February.... I snapped upright. Suddenly the day had my full attention. Tomorrow was Valentine's Day! How could I have missed it? Of course—it's too hot. Valentine's Day comes in the winter. This is not winter. No wonder I forgot. I was still out of sync with the seasons.

I began to plan. Tonight, after everyone is in bed, I'll make Valentine cards. Tomorrow, while they're in school, I'll bake a heart-shaped chocolate cake for dessert. We'll have a little celebration with passionfruit ice cream to go with the cake.

After the older ones were off to school, I called Pam and Jackie. "Mrs. Robinson is coming over on the boat. Would you like to go to the jetty with me to pick her up?"

"Oh, goodie!" Jackie squealed. "I like Mrs. Robinson. She's very nice and she likes pets. I do, too."

"Can we take our dolls?" Pam asked.

"Yes, but you must leave them in the car," I said firmly, laying down the ground rules. Fishing for dolls that have accidentally (question mark) fallen from the dock isn't my idea of fun.

We drove to the jetty and walked out on the pier just as the ferry came aorund the bend. "There's Mrs. Robinson!" Pam pointed to the boat.

"Where, where?" Jackie piped. I picked her up so she could see Hypatia waving from the deck.

"My goodness, how you two have grown in just a couple of months," Hypatia said, joining us on the deck.

"I brought my doll to meet you," Pam explained with an innocent look. "But she had to stay in the car so she wouldn't fall overboard." With that profound news, she and Jackie skipped on ahead.

"She's not quite as shy as she was," Hypatia smiled.

"No, and thank goodness she's not as talkative. She's five years old and very determined. Her dad jokes about her being the first woman premier of Australia. She likes to organize people, especially Jackie."

Hypatia laughed. "How does Jackie feel about that? She's three, isn't she?"

"Yes, and she can hold her own. Jackie has an entirely different personality than Pam. She never meets a stranger and has an uncanny way of understanding people at first sight. She loves animals and is always ready to help or rescue."

"Sounds like an interesting combination," Hypatia observed with a smile as we settled into the car. While I drove, she admired the dolls and listened to the history and behavior of each one. *Who taught them to be so informative?* I wondered. *They sound just like their mother.*

After Hypatia said 'G'day' to Bill, she held Topper and listened while the girls explained all his antics. Later, she suggested a walk around the farm. "It's such a beautiful day, and I'd love to see what you've been doing."

Hand in hand with the girls, we strolled through the fields discussing crops and farm work. Suddenly, Hypatia bent to scoop up a three-inch grasshopper and quickly snapped its head off. Seeing my look of horror, she explained, "It's an easy thing to do when you know that these critters can ruin your crops." I looked at this lovely, refined French woman and wondered if I would ever be able to do that.

After lunch, with Topper down for a nap and the girls outside playing, I brewed a pot of tea.

Hypatia, arranging the tea tray, marveled, "Pam and Jackie are quite a pair. They're so compatible it's hard to tell where one leaves off and the other begins."

"You're right," I agreed as we moved into the living room to relax with our tea. "They often move in unison and say the same words at the same time. We call them Miss Curiosity and Miss Friendly. And Miss Mischief is their leader. What one doesn't think of, the other one does. Last month they decided to teach the baby ducklings to swim by holding them under water. Of course, the results were fatal. A hard lesson was learned that day." I shook my head, thinking of the sadly departed baby ducks.

Just then, our dynamic duo burst into the room. "The kitten fell down!" they shouted in unison.

"Where is the kitten?" I asked, suspecting the worst.

Looking down at the floor, Pam said in a subdued voice, "In the privy." She peeked up briefly to see how I would react. Our privy sets over a ten-foot-deep hole.

"Go find your dad," I instructed them. "He'll get the kitten out." After they left, I explained to Hypatia that rescuing kittens from the privy was not my department. "I just don't have the stomach for those things."

A few moments later, Bill poked his head in with a report. "I lassoed the kitten and pulled it out. It's all right, but it's quite a mess."

Hypatia jumped up. "I'll clean the kitty," she told Bill. Looking at me, she smiled sympathetically. "You don't have to come, I can handle it."

"Thank God for people with strong stomachs." I sighed, remembering the grasshopper. I looked at the clock. The day had flown by. It was time to fix after-school snacks. I laid out cookies and milk. I could hear the children down in the yard. They had arrived home and were visiting with Hypatia. When I looked out, I saw Mickey huddled with Pam and Jackie, lecturing them on what not to do to kittens.

With the kitty fresh and clean, it was time for Hypatia to leave for the boat. "I'll drive her down to the jetty and bring Rusty back," I told Bill. "The children have already had their snack and Mickey is taking care of Topper."

As we headed down the hill, Hypatia noted how grown up Tia had become. "She acts like a young lady. How old is she now?"

"She's eight. It's surprising the things she can do when

The Way Things Are

she wants to. She has a knack for fashion and design. We have a lot of fun making doll clothes. She draws a picture to show me what she wants. She's good at entertaining Jackie and Pam with stories she makes up. I often see them crowded into her bed listening with rapt attention to her latest tale. When she switched her focus to Topper, they were quite upset about having to share her attention."

"I don't blame them," Hypatia sympathized. "She does seem very protective of them, though."

"Yes, she's a wonderful help. She keeps an eye on them while we're in the fields—with Pam and Jackie, that's no easy job."

"I can imagine!" Hypatia laughed as we walked along the jetty. "How is Rusty doing with his change from boarding school?"

"He's delighted to be at home. He manages our twenty-nine ducks and seventeen chickens. In his spare time, he tries to spear-fish like the aborigines. He made his own spear gun and actually manages to get fish. He keeps his rifle handy for his self-appointed task of ridding the farm of pests—especially chicken hawks and poisonous snakes. Quite a change from boarding school."

"Sounds like he is a handy young man to have around." After a pause, Hypatia added, "You have a wonderful family. Don't worry about the little girls. They do grow up."

I laughed as the boat pulled into the dock and thanked her again for cleaning the kitten. The quiet jetty suddenly sprang into life as the high schoolers climbed off the boat. Rusty had just a few minutes to visit with Hypatia before the passengers were handed on board. We waved goodbye and headed along the jetty toward home.

"How was your day?" I asked Rusty.

"I got to play baseball. The bases were loaded and I hit a home run! It was a great game," he said, excited about his feat. There was a short pause, and then, "Mom, how do you talk to girls?"

"What do you mean?"

"Well, what do you talk about? I mean, how do you start?"

You could make a comment about one of your classes or the weather."

"Boys and girls aren't supposed to mix at school. I found out it's a rule. I don't think it's a good rule, do you?"

"It's certainly not the way it's done in the States, but I suppose the rule is for a good reason. Sometimes boys get so involved with girls they end up neglecting a lot of other important things. Like schoolwork or fishing, or hunting, or ball games, and lots of other things boys enjoy."

"I guess that's right," he said, relieved. "By the way, Bob Stockwell is coming over Saturday in his rowboat. Can I go fishing with him?"

You'll have to check with Dad. he may need you for a few hours to finish the planting. Did you say Bob is going to row over here in a rowboat? That's a heroic four-mile trip! Does his mother know?"

"Yes, he's done it before, lots of times. He has a twelve-foot boat. Bob likes to hunt and fish, like I do. He told me that fishing isn't what it used to be, years ago, before the farms used poison sprays. But he said once you learn the wind and tides, you're bound to catch something, even if it's only a shark."

"I'll settle for some whiting or bream, thank you. You can do the driving," I said, sliding over to the passenger seat.

Chapter Sixteen

Unsung Heroes

SATURDAY MORNING BILL AND RUSTY finished the planting while Mickey helped me with inside chores. His biggest objection: he hates the washing machine as much as I do. We often get our fingers caught in the wringer. I knew what was coming when I heard the angry banging downstairs.

Mickey stormed into the kitchen frowning. "Mom! The release lever is on top of the rollers. When my fingers get caught I bash them even more by pounding on the lever!"

"I'm sorry,." I soothed him. "You're a hero for surviving the battle with that washing machine. Come, let me put something on your hand. I'll be down to hang out the clothes as soon as I finish the dishes. After that, Dad and I are going to help the Routledges while Topper takes his nap. Would you mind watching the girls for me? Rusty's going fishing with Bob?"

"Okay, I'll be cleaning my room anyway. I want to change it around."

"Again," I said, remembering last week. He had moved everything into the living room to rearranged them item by item. "You have the makings of an interior decorator or an architect." He smiled as I patted him on the shoulder. "Do you know where Skippy is? I want to let him know we're leaving."

"No, I haven't seen him for quite a while."

Where can he be? I wondered. Eleven-year-old Skippy marches to the beat of a different drum. He grasps cold facts concerning math or studies, but stays vague about cold facts concerning life. He prefers to be dangerously courageous. Usually he acts slow and deliberately, but in an emergency, he moves with the speed of lightening.

"Does anyone know where Skippy is?" I asked the girls.

"I saw him go up the hill," Pam said, glancing in that direction. Pam always knows what's going on and where people are.

Just then, he came running down the hill wearing shorts and no shirt. I walked up to meet him. He had a hunting knife with a four inch blade hanging on a string around his neck. I was tempted to scold. Instead, I calmly explained where we were going, and that he was to stay at home.

"Righto, Mom."

"By the way, where have you been?"

"Down at the water."

"What's the knife for?"

"To protect myself," he explained with a grin.

"Skippy," I said, looking directly into his eyes, "it is very dangerous to run with a knife hanging around your neck. If you fell, you could kill yourself. I don't want you to ever do that again." Recognizing my mother-means-it voice, he looked solemn. "Yes, Ma'am," he said.

A long time later, I learned that he had swum across the shark-frequented waters to Stradbroke. The knife was in case he met a shark. I thanked God for watching over my children. A "shark battle" hero was not the kind we were looking for.

With the planting done and the children in school, Bill turned his attention to the house roof that was beginning to rust. "I think I had better get that roof painted while I can," he said, peering up at the sky. "It looks like we're going to crop a bit of bad weather."

The weather didn't improve and the wind grew stronger. About midday I climbed the ladder. Peeking over the roof's edge, with my "please" voice, I suggested that he could finish the roof later. "I'll only be a little while," he assured me firmly. "I'm almost done."

"It's awfully windy," I said, trying to convince him.

"I'm not going to blow off," he said confidently. There was nothing else I could do but pray.

Back inside, I noticed that the wind was gusting hard. Blowing under the house and up through thin cracks between the floor boards, it was lifting the kitchen lino. I turned on the radio hoping to get a weather report. I heard: "A cyclone is bearing down on the east coast of Australia..." That was enough to send me outside to demand that Bill get down from the roof. Luckily, he had finished and was putting the ladder away.

Over lunch, I told him about the storm. "As soon as I eat I had better go down and check on the boat," he said. "If it drifts, it may get into the Mangrove swamp and break up by being blown against those roots."

"Be careful," I cautioned as he started off. "Don't do anything dangerous." It was like talking to the wind, as my grandmother used to say. I knew he was looking forward to another adventure.

By the time he reached the jetty, the boat had already drifted a quarter of a mile down the bay. It was up against a small mango-stump island. Bill hopped into his eight foot dinghy and rowed to the boat. He secured it to the dinghy and started to tow it back. It would have been easier if he could have cranked up the engine and motored back, but the engine was not working. We had been too busy planting to deal with the boat. Pushing against the wind and tide, it took him four hours to row 300 feet back into the cove. Another unsung hero.

Meanwhile, back at the house, I was pacing a groove in the floor between the kitchen and the window that looks out on the driveway. I had involved the children in jobs and projects, trying not to let them know how worried I was. Finally, I heard the wonderful, welcomed sound of the tractor in the driveway.

After the excitement of Bill arriving home and hearing his story about the boat, my anxiety level returned to normal. With great thankfulness we fell into bed exhausted and slept through the night. We were too worn out to hear the cyclone that dumped ten inches of water on the island.

The next morning we went out to evaluate the storm's damage. It had knocked over some banana trees, and washed out a lot of our turnip crop. We were moaning over the loss of our crops, when the boys came rushing home. "You should see Mr. Capper's house," Rusty said. "The roof blew off." The whole island turned out when they heard the news. Some to watch and some to help with repairs.

Serious as it was, the heavy rain gave us an opportunity to catch up on long deferred projects. The first priority was beaching the boat for repairs. "We may not get to it right away," Bill said, "but, at least, it is up high and dry."

Chapter Seventeen

Going Places and Doing Things

With our farm running more smoothly, we decided to try some of the organizational meetings. I attended Country Women's Association on the first Wednesday of each month. Bill and I went to the Parent's and Citizen's Association meeting on the third Monday of each month and visited the R.K.L.M. Horticultural Society on the second Friday of each month.

We met the same people at each of the meetings. "They amaze me," I told Bill. "They keep the current meeting separate from all other meetings. I never hear them discussing ideas or issues from Monday at a Wednesday, or Friday meeting. It may be an unwritten law."

"Could be," Bill said. "At least I'm getting lots of tips on farming and the meetings are keeping us current on island affairs."

"Yes, and your Aunt Jac is keeping us currant with what's happening in the rest of the world. It's so peaceful here we're inclined to forget all the strife going on out there."

"Too right." he grinned. "When she sends the *Down Easter* magazine from Maine it makes me want to head back to snow country."

"Fair dinkum?" I wanted to know.

"Not really," he said with a shrug. "When I think of shoveling all that stuff, I get over it."

I gave him a quick hug thinking of his fond memories of growing up in Maine. "There are times when the older children would like to be in the States, too," I said. "Especially when they look at the toy catalogs Aunt Jac sends. They love showing the Australians all the things that can be bought in America. Personally, I don't think the newer toys leave anything to a child's imagination. Press a button and the toy does it all."

"Who needs them," Bill chided. "When we were growing up we made our own toys."

"Speaking of toys," Rusty interrupted, walking in on the conversation. "I just finished the girl's sand box. Can I take the tractor down to the other end of the island to get some sand to put in it?"

"See what I mean?" Bill chuckled, giving Rusty a go-ahead nod. "Toys are just one more blessing of farm life. Almost anything the kids really want they can create from what's available."

Bill was right. When Topper outgrew his playpen Mickey built him an enclosed area next to the chicken yard. He used chicken wire and four-foot posts that we had on hand. Next he made a little six-inch high platform to satisfy

Topper's urge to climb. A few weeks later, he asked if he could add a rod for him to swing from when he was ready. "All boys like to climb and swing from things," he said. Topper loved his new play yard and soon made friends with the chickens. We often heard him talking to them—using what sounded like perfect chicken language.

Topper and chicken

Mickey's next project was a lookout tower up in the woods. It was an eight-foot square platform on four, huge ten-foot posts. He made it all by himself, from the post holes up. It was still standing after months of hard use. "You can't buy a toy like that in a catalog." Bill said proudly.

"As long as he doesn't fall off," this typical mother murmured.

Tia's project was a lot safer. She began sewing table napkins by hand. Very carefully she decorated them with embroidery stitches learned at school. "They match the green table cloth," she said proudly. "I made a napkin for everyone, even Topper."

Very good!" I praised her. I was determined that even though we lived on an island, proper table manners were still important. After our shipment arrived from the States, we decided to use tablecloths, bone china and cloth napkins at dinner time.

"Which side does the fork go on?" was asked so often I made a table-setting poster with circles and lines for plates, silverware and glasses. I hung it on the dining room wall for a quick reference. We ate together as a family—a wonderful advantage to living on a farm. No one ate until the food was blessed. No one left the table until the thanksgiving prayer was said.

Table conversation released the day's tensions. I often entertained everyone with bits of stories I had read, and they shared their experiences. We encouraged them to talk about their day, with an ear tuned to hurts and frustrations. Some of the best times were when we lingered at the end of a meal. Fed and relaxed, difficulties that couldn't be talked about earlier come to the surface. Issues of life were discussed and settled. Very often sympathy, or problem solving, came from a brother or sister who had coped with a similar situation.

It was easier to teach a moral lesson, or counsel, without pointing a finger at anyone in particular. Family mealtimes were one of our most valuable tools for raising well-rounded adults. It was at the table that family responsibility developed and grew. Sharing at meals taught them to care for each other.

That reminds me, no housework today—only the important things. Sort out the box of stray keys for Bill. Make a bead necklace for Tia for her friend's birthday. Put curlers in the doll's hair for Pam. Sew the eyes back on Jackie's teddy bear. Make a sheath for Skippy's hunting knife. Help Mickey with his latest floor plans. And—untangle Rusty's fishing line that Topper thought was his.

Chapter Eighteen

Stepping Out at Easter Time

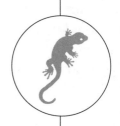

OUR NEXT AUSTRALIAN TRANSITION WAS AT Easter. "What can we do to celebrate Easter when there is no church to attend?" I challenged Bill.

"We could have an Easter Egg Hunt for the island children," he suggested.

"That's a jolly good idea," I said, "but we need something else."

"How about visiting someone in the afternoon?"

"Who can we visit?" I asked.

"I don't know, the Routledges? The Russells?"

"Well, we see them all the time. I want this to be different."

"What about the Slieps?" he said tentatively.

"That's a great idea. The children need to relate to older people. The Slieps are in their early 70s and live on the other side of the island. That should make the day special."

"Fair enough!" Bill said, "Mr. Sliep is partly responsible for our being here. Remember? He was featured in the newspaper article that introduced us to Russell Island. His wife, Mrs. Sliep, was a nurse in England during the first World War. She's still a spunky lady. But, I've heard that she hasn't been well lately and doesn't get around much."

"Oh," I grimaced, "do you think they would want to bother entertaining us, with seven children?"

"Well, there's no harm in asking," he said. "If they can't we could try the De Vrooms or the Hollands. Those three families have the oldest people on the island. Perhaps we should try all three so that no one will be offended."

With great apprehension I called each family to ask if we could come to say hello and wish them Happy Easter. I explained that it would be a brief visit. *After all—who wants to entertain seven children any longer than briefly?* I thought to myself. Surprisingly, they all seemed delighted with the idea. Oddly enough all three families were Dutch.

Confidence restored, I started to make preparations for the Easter Egg Hunt. "Eggs," I wailed, "We forgot, this is molting season. Eggs are hard to come by this time of year!"

"Fair dinkum, " Bill said, "I'll give it a go. Perhaps we can borrow some. I'll talk to the blokes at the jetty."

"You sound like an Australian. What do you mean 'fair dinkum'?" I teased.

"I mean really, I'll ask some of the guys at the jetty," he huffed.

Eventually, we collected five dozen eggs from here and there. When they heard what we were planning, the Routledges, Pointons, Miss Watts, Jack Wynn and the Russells all contributed.

I ran the primus all evening to make hard boiled eggs for our coloring session the next day. The girls and I spent the afternoon decorating eggs with cups of dye, crayons and lots of imagination. "Watch out for Topper," I cautioned scooping him up as he reached for one of the dye cups.

"Look at what he did to the crayons!" Tia moaned. "They're all over the floor."

"Mickey," I called, holding the squirming culprit. "Would you play with Topper outside for a while?"

After the eggs were finished we fashioned Easter baskets from construction paper. We shredded green tissue paper for grass. The next day, we tucked in a little decorated cake as a gift for each of the three families.

Sunday morning was a beautiful autumn day. Clear and sunny, it was just right for an Easter Egg Hunt. Children from littles to teenagers arrived from all over the island. We hid eggs in the paddock and front yard for the little ones, and everywhere else for the older ones. The Australian children weren't sure what to do at first but were soon caught up in the excitement of a new custom.

"I think we started something," Bill said, laughing as he watched them scurrying around. After refreshments we awarded prizes for each age group and sent everyone home with a treat.

It was time to dress the children in what Bill called Sunday-go-to-meeting clothes. Dainty dresses over stiff crinolines, hats, gloves and purses for the girls. The boys looked handsome in polished shoes, dress pants, white shirts and ties. We wanted them to know that life is more than bare feet and play clothes.

"Who should we visit first?" I asked Bill.

"Well, Slieps are farthest away so we probably should start there."

The Slieps greeted us cordially and invited us to join them for afternoon tea. I looked at Bill with raised eyebrows. "I didn't expect all this," my eyes said. Bill responded with a gentle nod that assured me, "It's okay."

The table was beautifully set with bone china. Besides the tea there were cookies, candies and fruits. How could we refuse? The children, bless them, behaved just the way well-trained children should. A pleasant hour passed before the Slieps allowed us to leave.

Settling into the car I breathed a sigh of relief. "They really seemed to enjoy us, didn't they?" I asked, amazed.

"Yes, I was surprised," Bill said. Looking over his shoulder, he shouted above the noise of the car, "You children were very good. I'm proud of you."

"So am I," I echoed. "But I had no idea we would be there so long. We'll have to make our next visit shorter."

We hurried on past the store to De Vroom's farm. Again we were warmly welcomed to a tea-table spread with cakes, cookies, candies and fruits. Beautiful music from Joe's classic record collection played in the background. Mrs. De Vroom, ninety-four-years-old, lived with her son Joe. She spoke with a heavy Dutch accent. A gracious lady from the old school. I found it hard to understand her, but Joe thoughtfully interpreted for us.

When Topper became restless with all the visiting, the boys took him outside for a walk. The girls stayed to charm Joe and his mother. Time passed much too quickly. Finally, remembering that we had another stop, I made eye contact with Bill. He nodded and stood up.

It was late afternoon before we arrived at the Hollands. Mrs. Holland, who will be ninety this year, lives with Alfie, her fifty-year-old son. He told us that every Thursday they fished together out in the boat.

Tiny Mrs. Holland was not happy with us. We were scolded for coming after the tea hour had passed. She invited us in, "but only for a short visit," she said. She was determined to get her share of the "proper" tea hour and made us vow to return the next afternoon. After promising we headed for the car. I warned Bill, "Tomorrow we had better mind our "P's" and "Q's" and arrive at the proper tea time."

Once in the car, I exclaimed, "Weren't they all wonderful people? They were so nice, and to go to all that trouble! Imagine inviting us back—with seven children, too."

I turned to the children, "Did you have a good afternoon?" I asked. They all spoke at once. When the din subsided we agreed that it had been an unforgettable Easter experience. Little did we realize that we had started a tradition.

The following week we returned to see Mrs. Holland at the "proper" tea time. Alfie took Bill and the boys out in the boat, while Mrs. Holland fussed over Topper and the girls. We had a wonderful time and won Mrs. Holland's forgiveness and approval.

Autumn flew by as we busied ourselves with the potato harvest. We had twenty rows waiting to be dug. "How will we ever finish the crop by using a tire iron to pry the potatoes out?" I wondered.

"We don't have to," Bill said.

I groaned. OK, here we go again. Twenty questions. "Why not?"

"Because, Curtis told me that if we use a moldboard

plow, we can turn the earth over so that the potatoes are setting right on top."

"Fair dinkum! But we don't have a moldboard plow."

"No, but Mr. Orme does and he said I could borrow it."

I was elated. Bill plowed a row and the whole family gathered the potatoes. We piled them into the little truck Bill had adapted for farm use. After they were washed with the irrigation hose we put them into burlap sacks. My job was to hold the sack open while Bill and the boys filled it.

One day, Bill came back from visiting Sergio. He was excited. "Guess what," he said.

"What?"

"Sergio made a frame with hooks to hold the potato sack while he fills it. He showed me how to do it." Another great leap in the potato business! My job shifted to sewing up the sacks with twine using a six-inch needle.

As the school year drew to a close, sadly the Grahams announced that they would be leaving in December. They had accepted a teaching position at Bamaga, an island off the top of Cape York Peninsular. The whole island was distressed by the news. School Break Up Day was not the same. Even the Christmas party was different. During the year, Jacksonville Hall had been struck by lightening and burned down. Festivities were held in the smaller Parish Hall at the jetty.

In January we were introduced to Mr. Wolfe, the new head teacher. With his wife and children, he moved into the house the Grahams had vacated. Rusty started his second year traveling on the school boat. Pam joined the others as a first grader in the island school.

Jackie was at a loss. She had never been without her best friend. Topper tried to fill the void. But it seemed that life for Jackie would never be the same. Bill and I tried to involve her in what we were doing as much as possible, often reminding her that next year she would be big enough to go to school!

Chapter Nineteen

The Winds of Change

BILL TOOK US WITH HIM WHEN HE WENT down to the store to pick up supplies from the noon boat. We got there early. I asked Jackie and Topper if they wanted to walk down to the jetty with me. By now, walking was a breeze. "Let's go play in the sand." Jackie coaxed. Topper didn't wait for an answer, he just headed for the water.

"Jolly good, that's a great idea." I said, grabbing him. "Let's take off our shoes first," I suggested. We waded in the water and made sand castles. We drew our names in the sand and watched the waves carry them away.

What a wonderful life I thought. Here we are romping on the beach in the middle of a work week. It was a wonderful day, warm and beautiful. The bay was calm—and so were we. Russell Island was our home. We knew the people. They had accepted us. We borrowed farm equipment from each other. We were members of their many organizations.

Actually, there were so many meetings going on, signals often got mixed. Mickey and I used to daydream about an island newspaper to keep us informed. "What we really need," I told him, "is a newspaper to cover all the islands."

When the school bought a new duplicator, Mickey seized the opportunity. He suggested that the School Project Club print an island newspaper. The new head teacher, Mr. Wolfe, was less than enthusiastic but gave the club permission. Mickey was chosen to be the editor.

"Mom!" he called, running up the steps from school. "we have four kids who are going to be reporters."

"Reporters for what?" I asked, playing the twenty questions game.

"Mr. Wolfe said we could do a newspaper."

"What kind of a newspaper?"

"For all the islands, like we talked about!"

"Great!" I was elated. "What are you going to call the newspaper?"

"We figured that out, too. It's for all the islands Russell, Karragarra, Lamb and Macleay. So we're calling it the R.K.L.M. NEWS. Now we have to find things to write about. Do you have any ideas?"

"Check to see how it's done in the newspaper," I advised. "They write about events that have happened or are about to happen. They have recipes, helpful hints, poems and short stories. Your reporters will have to develop a nose for news."

"A nose for news! That can be our motto." Mickey jumped up and headed for his desk. Off to write the story of the year, I supposed.

Just before dinner, he emerged from his room waving the newspaper banner. Neatly printed across the top in his best tech-drawing lettering was *R.K.L.M. NEWS*. Below that, beside a picture of a pointer dog it said:

A NOSE FOR NEWS

Printed by the Russell Island State School Project Club. Price: 3¢

News of the islands, for the islands, will be delivered to your door each month by the R.K.L.M. NEWS. This service has been undertaken by the School Project Club. A staff of four reporters will be headed by the Editor, Michael Moore. We will scout the islands for the latest news, notices of entertainments and advertisements for your enjoyment and convenience. Any news or contributions will be gladly accepted by these reporters: Russell Island, Neville Holmes; Karragarra Island, Trevor Noyes; Lamb Island, Graham Noyes and Brian Kerr on Macleay Island.

"And look this," Mickey said. It was a report he had written on the progress being made to provide Russell Island with electricity. A possibility dear to his heart.

"Mickey, this is wonderful. The pointer dog is a great idea. How did you come up with that?"

"I found it in the rubber-stamp set. And, guess what, I

have a story by Rusty to put in our first issue. Want me to read it to you?"

I nodded. He began:

The Trout Fisher

I stood at the edge of the forest that gave way to a fast flowing stream, watching the trout fisher kneeling at the edge of a pool. His eyes portrayed a knowledge and pride of his sport, although it came as instinct.

His hair was uncombed and ruffled by the wind. From head to foot he was about six feet of heavy build. His face was that of a laughing school boy when in good humor.

There he knelt, his large, massive body hunched, looking intently into the water watching. Watching. Waiting. Down crashed his hairy arm into the water, up flashed a plump gleaming trout. He sat on his haunches surveying his prize with laughing eyes. There on the ground lay the meal of the Trout Fisher, better known as the Grizzly Bear.

–R. Moore

I looked up. Rusty stood in the doorway. "You wrote that?" I asked.

"Yes, Ma'am." A slow grin hid in the corners of his mouth waiting for my response.

"It's terrific!" I exclaimed. "So well written, and with a very clever twist. I can't wait to see it in print." The grin came out of hiding and splashed across his face. Proudly I told him, "I can see we have another writer in the family, keep it up.

"By the way, Dad and I have been invited to Ron and Jack's for dinner tonight. I've made dinner for the family and you're in charge until we get back."

We had met Ron and Jack just before the Grahams left. New on the island, they had been owners of an antique store in Wollongong, New South Wales. Their house was furnished with antiques. Beautiful pieces of pottery, fine paintings, chairs, small tables and—Mickey's favorite, a German cuckoo clock.

"This is an opportunity to dress up." I told Bill, excited with the idea. I wore a dress with hose, heels and gloves as though we were going to a fancy restaurant. Australian ladies wear gloves to go shopping in the city, why not to dinner? Sometimes my heart has to know that there is still a civilization out there and that I am still a part of it.

Ron and Jack, more cosmopolitan than most of the islanders, appreciated my effort to make the evening special. At dinner we discussed our travels and world news. Eventually our conversation drifted to the island newcomers. "I was down at the jetty when Leo Grosse arrived." Jack said. "Before he tied up at the jetty, he put on a good show zooming around the bay doing figure eights in his fancy speed boat."

"That's right," Ron frowned, "He boasted about how much he had paid for the boat and bragged about how rich he was. But he doesn't look, or act, the part of a rich speed-boat owner."

"Yes," Jack said, as he collected the first course plates and headed for the kitchen. "Word is going around that he's a 'Collins Street Farmer.'"

"What's a 'Collins Street Farmer?'" Bill asked.

"It's someone who has been hired to babysit a tax-deduction property for some rich lawyer in Sydney," Ron explained. "But no one seems to know the real facts."

Returning with the dinners Jack added, "He's been hard on the boat skippers. On his way back to Redland Bay he cruises away from the jetty just before the regular launch arrives. Usually taking several of their paying passengers."

"He has a foul mouth, too," Ron said, shaking his head. "And I don't like the idea of his inviting the teens over to his house and offering them beer and wine."

"Goodness," I said. "For a while, we allowed Pam to play with his youngest daughter. Then Pam began swearing and telling lies. We wondered where she learned such things."

"Well, time will tell," Ron said with a sigh. "Although most of the islanders are agog over this flashy fellow we've decided to reserve judgment for a while."

Bill and I agreed. The conversation turned to happier things. "Did you get your copy of the *R.K.L.M. NEWS?*" I asked.

They both nodded. "Mickey gave us one today," Jack said. "He told me it was printed in purple ink because of the school's new mimeograph machine."

"The reporters did a great job garnering news and announcing events," Ron marveled. "I appreciated the club meeting times and church notices. We don't always get all the grapevine news."

Bill chuckled, "I like the poems, jokes and little stories. Kids have great imaginations."

"Too right,," Jack said, "I think the *R.K.L.M. NEWS* is going to be a great success.

We didn't realize it at the time but the June issue held two items that were to change our lives. Sergio Vladovitch was bidding Russell Island goodbye. He had sold his house. "There goes our church." I told Bill sadly. "We'll miss Sergio. He was a good neighbor."

The last item on the page welcomed the new family who had bought Sergio's farm. The Grosses had three children, the article said. Thorton, the oldest, would be going over on the high-school boat. The two girls, Lulu and Evelyn, would attend the Russell Island school. The arrival of this family heralded a great change for the island, and its people.

It was soon apparent that our new neighbor and the new head teacher did not like Americans. A wave of anti-Americanism began to stir. Probably inspired by *The Ugly American*, a book that was popular in the early '60s.

The children were harassed at school with unspoken approval from the teacher. Indeed, he often joined in to provoke Mickey. Finally, Mickey asked to be withdrawn as newspaper editor and team captain.

"It's not worth all the fighting," he complained when he came home.

I put my arm around his shoulder, "I know you're discouraged. I guess I would be, too. But don't let it get you down. Just remember, you started something that is so good, it will continue. No matter what happens, we will always know that the newspaper was your idea. You'll have a lot of other challenges in life and interesting things to do. You're right about this. It isn't worth the fighting, especially if you end up fighting the teacher."

"But, Mom, why is everyone changing so? We used to be good friends with all the islanders. But ever since the Grahams left and the Grosse family came, things seem to be different."

The newspaper limped along and was eventually taken over by the P&C, (Parents and Citizens Association). Later, it was renamed and published at Redland Bay. It was sad to see our dream die but we were proud that Mickey, the American, originated what had become a tradition, not only on the islands, but also in the bay area.

After dinner that evening, Bill and I decided to go for a walk. I sighed, as we started down the road. "I really need a breath of fresh air tonight," I said wearily.

"I knew you were upset, what's the matter?"

"It's the way the teacher is behaving toward our children, especially Mickey."

"Mmm," Bill murmured. "Waiting for the mail at the jetty, I've heard a lot of disturbing things about our new neighbors. It's almost as though a black cloud is gathering on the horizon."

"Oh no," I wailed. "Just when we were getting along so well. I wish the Grahams were still here. They were such a stabilizing influence to the island."

"Yes, they were. But it seems as though this new fellow is just the opposite." He took a deep breath. Moments passed. "Time will tell," he said softly.

Chapter Twenty

The Birthdays

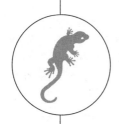

THE HENS, WHO HAD BEEN TAKING A vacation, suddenly started laying eggs. So many, we had to find clever ways to use them. Like mixing a dozen into a bread pudding made with whole wheat bread and lots or raisins. It was one recipe that our wood-stove oven could not spoil.

"What else can we do with the eggs?" I asked the children one afternoon. "Any suggestions?"

"How about making a cake for Mrs. Holland's birthday?" Rusty said. "Alfie told us she'll ninety years old tomorrow."

"Good idea, Rusty. Want to help me make the cake?"

"Righto, I'll get some wood and start a fire in the stove."

"I'm going to make a card." Tia said, running off to the craft table in the sun room. Pam and Jackie scrambled on chairs beside her ready to offer advice and assistance. Seeing the direction this project was going to take, I set colored paper in front of Pam and Jackie.

"Here, girls, why don't you each make a card for Mrs. Holland. She would like that." Bursting with importance, they busied themselves while Rusty and I made the birthday cake.

The next day, all dressed up, and gingerly balancing the decorated cake, the girls and I climbed into the car. The car wouldn't start. "Oh, no," Tia wailed, "what can we do? We can't carry the cake all the way to Hollands. We'll be all dirty when we get there." The Hollands lived about two miles away. A long dusty walk on a hot day.

"Get Daddy and the tractor." Pam piped up.

"That's a good idea but Dad is working up in the fields. We'd get just as dirty trying to find him. Perhaps if we push the car up the hill a little bit, I might be able to start it when it rolls down."

Jackie, always ready for a challenge, strode towards the car with determination. "I can push hard." She said.

I didn't want to tell her she was too little, so I suggested, "We need you to be our lookout. Stand right over there while we push. Let us know if we push too far."

With Jackie stationed at her important post, we were able to move the car up the little hill near the road. I put the brake on, and cautioned the girls to stay behind the car and give it a shove when I raised my hand. They pushed and I pumped the gas.

I must have been watching them rather than where I was coasting. Crash! down went a fencepost—but the car had started. Everyone climbed aboard. We were off to Mrs. Holland's. She was delighted with the cake, the cards, and our visit. She sent us home with happy hearts. What's a fencepost when you can be a blessing to someone?

When Bill came down from the farm he found me scribbling on a tablet in the quiet of the Gazebo. "What are you doing?" he asked.

"I'm answering Aunt Jac's letter. She wanted to know how the farm was going and how the children were getting along."

"Well, I'll go finish up," he said. He paused, "... by the way, do you know what happened to the fencepost out front?"

"Do you know how hard it is to get that car started?" I asked looking straight at him.

"Oh," he smiled. "Go back to your writing." I nodded. Collecting my thoughts, I began to write…

Dear Aunt Jac,

Thanks for your letter. We always enjoy your news, though it's hard to relate to Maine's cold weather when it's so hot and sunny down here. After reading about all the snow you've had, I'm happy we didn't retire up there. We've been spoiled by living in subtropical climates for so many years.

The children were delighted that you liked the birthday card they made. It's hard to explain eighty-one years of age to young ones, so I tried using inches. They were awed, and asked when I would be eighty-one inches high. I told them I didn't have time to work on it right now, the farm kept me too busy.

For a while, we felt like total failures as farmers. Bill worked from dawn to dusk and made about a dollar a day—before deductions. At least we learned a lot about what not to do. Since then, we have steadily improved our farm and it's management by inventing better ways to do things.

We had a wonderful piece of luck planting twenty rows of sweet potatoes very early in the season. They drew the highest market prices. Fortunately they sold at just the right time. We were through the elbows and knees of our work pants and shirts. Prosperity smiled when we were able to buy six sets of new work clothes.

Our biggest morale booster was "the ladybug." It started life in the late 50s as one of those neat little foreign Vanguard sedans. It came to us with a badly crumpled fender and no headlights for only $40. Just ten dollars more than the cost of a wheel barrow.

Mickey used a coal chisel to slice across the roof above the front windshield. Bill and the boys lifted the entire back section off with it's cushioned seats. They placed it on the truck bed of our old Rackety Boom. One cold day, looking for a sunny place to sit, I climbed up on the truck and relaxed in the cozy back seat of the Vanguard. The view from that height was great. The seat was comfortable and the windows and roof provided shelter from the weather. We dubbed this contrivance "The Gazebo."

The Gazebo soon became part of our Sunday ritual. Sunday is barge day for Monday's Farmer's Market. Even though we have to take our produce down to the jetty in the afternoon, we try to make the morning special. After Bible reading and a prayer time, Bill cooks his famous pancakes. I create a tropical fruit compote of paw paw, bananas and any other fruit available. By the way, over here we can't buy maple syrup. Australia's Golden Syrup is much thicker and made from sugar cane. Either way, pancakes and fruit compote are pronounced "Sunday."

When we finish our leisurely breakfast the children take over the kitchen and clean up. Bill and I retire to the Gazebo for some well earned quiet time. Sitting in cozy comfort, we put our heads together to solve all the world's problems as well as our own. Complaints and interruptions are met with—"Not now. Mom and Dad are talking."

What did we do with the rest of the car? Well, by now, all we had was the front of the car with the engine and frame. Bill and Mickey built a flat wooden platform on the frame to serve as a truck body and driver's seat. Bill, who is becoming a very clever carpenter, added detachable sides all around to hold the crops when we harvest. He also made a removable rack for shifting the twenty-foot lengths of irrigation pipe. Small enough to drive along the rows, this blessed little vehicle goes all over the farm toting anything and everything. It saves us many a weary step and wasted hour.

You would laugh at the gas tank. It's a gallon can with a hose to the carburetor. A car headlight, secured in a box and clipped to the battery, serves as a headlight at night.

When it's dark Mickey drives. Skippy sits on the front fender shining the light on the road. That is, until he hears a wallaby hopping by in the bush. Then he lights up the woods and the road disappears. Mickey yells, jerking him back to attention just before they run off the road.

To stop the truck when the brakes won't work, they turn off the motor and coast up a hill. A push down the hill gets it started again. Although they dream of something better, they do love the challenge of this little vehicle.

After all our struggles you'll be pleased to hear about our crops. We've already planted 200 rows of sweet potatoes. We plan to do more during the off season on the warmest section of our farm—now that we know where the warmest section is. We're always hoping that this year will be "our" year.

We did get five inches of rain in one week, the best we've had all season. It softened the ground enough for us to dig up small avocado trees from Mr. De Vroom's farm. We plan to start our own grove. Imagine, a tree that doesn't have to be sprayed!

Bill loathes poisonous concoctions. We use all organic fertilizers and avoid things that require spray as much as possible. You wouldn't believe how much poison is on the average tomato. It will take four to seven years for the avocados to become full-bearing, but when they do we should be fairly secure. We may turn out to be farmers after all!

Rusty is a great help on the farm. He's just a tad taller than I am with broad shoulders like his dad. Even though he's more interested in fishing, boats and girls, in that order, he does do well on his exams. He'll sit for his Junior Public Exam at the end of the year. The equivalent of our sophomore year in the States. Most Australian teens leave school at that point for jobs or apprenticeships. Rusty will continue on to Senior.

Mickey has been pouring over house plans in the magazines you send, always wanting more details. Up until now, his focus was interior design, but his interest in architecture is growing. Otherwise, he's an obnoxious fourteen-year-old who has discovered "The Great Truth": His parents are hopelessly old fashioned! Fortunately, he is not a moody child. His good humor quickly returns. An enterprising boy, Mickey already has a part-time job on another farm.

Skippy is at the top of his class and much harder to understand. He's always been his father's boy and works well with him when the other boys are busy. And, like his dad, he's great at sports.

Blonde-headed Tia is a typical nine-year-old and second in her grade at school. Her favorite class is sewing. Hand-sewing is taught in Australian schools from the first grade on. She makes a lot of little things with my sewing machine. I taught her to use the machine turning the wheel by hand with the power off. When she has had enough practice keeping her fingers away from the needle, I'll let her use it with the power on.

Pam is the most curious of all our children. For as long as I can remember, she has had a pencil in her hand. She devours school in great gulps, memorizing all the third grade poems as well as those of the first grade (an advantage of a two-room school system). At home she lines up her dolls and teaches them lessons she has "written" on her blackboard.

Jackie is lost with Pam away at school. They used to do everything together. What Pam didn't think of, Jackie did. Now that they're old enough to go off to play with friends I pin a note on the back of their clothes, 'Please send me home at 11:30.' It really works.

Precocious is probably the best word to describe Jackie. With her strawberry blond hair and a smattering of freckles she's hard to resist and is always busy thinking of things to do. I can't imagine what mischief she and Topper would get into, if he were old enough to have her freedom to roam. Fortunately, at two years old, we're able to keep him close to home.

Topper's a sturdy little mechanized blond. He seldom moves without turning on his motor. His "brrrmmm, brrmmm" can be heard all over the house. I say, "Come here Topper, I want to tuck in your shirt." He shifts himself into reverse gear to back up, sometimes it requires a three point maneuver—he does know the difference. Finally, he gets close enough to get his shirt taken care of. For such a little fellow, he is surprisingly neat and tidy, always ready to lend a helping hand. First he watches to see what needs to be done and then copies what he sees us do.

The children have made great progress since we've been here. At the end of last year's school concert, prizes were awarded for achievement. When the stage curtain opened, we were surprised to see that three of the six prize winners belonged to the Moore family! Sadly, the Grahams, who have been the children's teachers since we came to the island have been transferred. We miss them.

Summing up our important gains I would have to say these count most: warm earth beneath our feet, the blue sky overhead, and all the things money can't buy—health, happiness, contentment, pride of accomplishment, and good friends.

"How's it going?" Bill asked peering up at me.

"Goodness," I jumped, "Is it time to get dinner already?"

"We're starving," he said, helping me down from the Gazebo.